WHY DO
CATS
BURY THEIR
POOP?

WHY DO CATS BURY THEIR POOP?

More Than 200 Feline Facts,
Fallacies, and Foibles Revealed

MARGARET H. BONHAM
AND
D. CAROLINE COILE, PhD

STERLING

New York / London
www.sterlingpublishing.com

STERLING and the distinctive Sterling logo are
registered trademarks of Sterling Publishing Co., Inc.

Library of Congress Cataloging-in-Publication Data

Bonham, Margaret H.
  Why do cats bury their poop? : more than 200 feline facts, fallacies, and foibles
revealed / Margaret H. Bonham and D. Caroline Coile.
    p. cm.
  Includes index.
  ISBN 978-1-4027-5040-3
  1. Cats--Behavior--Miscellanea. 2. Cats--Miscellanea. I. Coile, D. Caroline. II. Title.
  SF446.5.B649 2008
  636.8--dc22
                                                              2008018841

10 9 8 7 6 5 4 3 2 1

Published by Sterling Publishing Co., Inc.
387 Park Avenue South, New York, NY 10016
© 2008 by Margaret H. Bonham and D. Caroline Coile, Ph.D.
Distributed in Canada by Sterling Publishing
c/o Canadian Manda Group, 165 Dufferin Street
Toronto, Ontario, Canada M6K 3H6
Distributed in the United Kingdom by GMC Distribution Services
Castle Place, 166 High Street, Lewes, East Sussex, England BN7 1XU
Distributed in Australia by Capricorn Link (Australia) Pty. Ltd.
P.O. Box 704, Windsor, NSW 2756, Australia

Sterling ISBN 978-1-4027-5040-3

For information about custom editions, special sales, premium
and corporate purchases, please contact Sterling Special Sales
Department at 800-805-5489 or specialsales@sterlingpublishing.com.

CONTENTS

1

THE CAT'S BODY

Do cats always land on their feet?

YES, UNLESS THEY LAND ON THEIR SIDE, back, or head. Obviously, if you hold your cat upside down a few inches over your bed, and let go, he's not going to have enough room or time to land on his feet. And he will not be amused by your experiment, even if you keep lifting him slightly higher until you find the magic distance at which he does, indeed, land on his feet. He may, in fact, be so unamused by this experiment that he will land on your face—but with his feet, of course, when you're sleeping, later on.

Beyond this magic distance, here's what happens. The cat's vestibular organ, located in his ear, tells the cat which way is up, and the first thing he does upon falling is to rotate his head until it's right-side up. Next, he rotates his front legs so they're close to his face and twists the upper part of his spine to be in line with his front legs and head. He then rotates his rear legs so they're parallel with his front legs, and his spine twists to come in line with his legs. Cats are able to maneuver like this in part because their skeletal system is extremely flexible, far more so than yours—even if you've attended yoga classes.

By the way, kittens first begin to show this ability when they're just four weeks old, and they perfect it by seven weeks of age. Try that with a baby (or better yet, don't)!

Just because cats land on their feet, though, doesn't mean they simply bounce up, unscathed. Try jumping from your roof and landing on your feet! You can do it, but depending on how high your roof is, it's going to hurt and maybe break some bones. Cats are the same way.

But wait—haven't some cats survived really incredible falls? Read on.... 🐾

Can cats survive a fall from a high-rise?

SOMETIMES. AS LONG AS THEY fall far enough. Huh? That's right. Cats have a bad habit of balancing on balcony railings or otherwise living life on the edge and, sometimes, fall off. Cats that fall from a two-story window can't cushion their fall adequately and their chins often hit the ground, hard, which can lead to some messed up teeth, or worse. The worse usually comes with slightly higher fall levels, where they are likely to break bones and rupture internal organs.

Then how is it that a cat is recorded as having survived a fall from a forty-sixth-story window? All right, to be fair, he did supposedly bounce off a canopy and into a planter. But then there was a cat that survived a twenty-story fall without benefit of canopy or planter. In fact, in a study of 187 cats that fell from high-rise windows (yes, there really was such a study, and no, it did not involve flinging cats out of windows at various heights) presumably on their own and were brought to a veterinary hospital for treatment, 90 percent survived after they had fallen an average of five-and-a-half stories. The weird thing is that more cats survived falls from above the seventh floor than from below it!

Researchers theorize that a cat's "terminal velocity" (there really is such a term) is not, actually, um, terminal as far as life is concerned. Terminal velocity is the maximum speed at which a falling object falls. The farther an object falls, the faster it goes, up to some limit at which the air resistance slows it to some maximum speed. A cat falling from a great height spreads its legs out so the loose skin acts as a sort of parachute, increasing wind resistance, like a flying squirrel. Sort of. The cat's terminal velocity is thought to be about sixty miles per hour, and researchers believe the cat reaches it after falling about five floors.

Now, this doesn't mean you should move to a higher floor and leave all your windows open. Nor does it mean you can hurl your cat from an airplane just to watch him parachute down (as one person is rumored to have done). Because there's one problem with this study: It was based on cats brought to the hospital following a fall. These cats were alive, presumably, when their owners scooped them up and took them for treatment. But also, presumably, the cats that had to be scooped up in a garbage pail were not taken to the kitty hospital but to the kitty morgue. These flat, splattered, and dismembered cats didn't get to be included in any statistics. So close your windows, and keep your cat off the balcony, no matter what floor you're on. You really don't want to find out what his terminal velocity is—even if he does land on his feet. 🐾

Do cats miss their claws when declawed?

FOR A LONG TIME, it's been very popular to have cats declawed to put an end to scratching. But do cats miss their claws when you declaw them? The answer may surprise you.

When declawing a cat, the veterinarian doesn't remove just a bit of the claw, but actually part of the toe, up to the first knuckle. After the surgery, the cat is in a fair amount of pain. Because part of the toe has been removed, the cat's balance is altered significantly and the cat may suffer pain from "phantom limbs." Indeed, you'll see cats that have been declawed still try to scratch at things.

If that weren't enough, many cat behaviorists believe that cats that are declawed have more behavioral problems than cats that keep their claws. Cat behaviorists tend to see declawed cats as problem pets that are more aggressive and that have more litter box problems.

Poor kitty! If you have a cat that scratches a lot, you should trim his nails and keep plenty of cat scratchers around the places he likes to scratch. What's more, you can put caps such as Soft Paws on your cat's nails to keep him from scratching up your furniture. 🐾

What's the purpose of that footpad way up at the top of the cat's wrist?

IF YOU FEEL BEHIND YOUR cat's front leg, up to where his foreleg meets his wrist, you'll find a footpad just like the ones on the bottom of your cat's feet. This pad, called the stopper pad (technically, the carpal pad), may seem to be in a strange place, way up there on the leg, until you see stop-action films of a cat running at high speed. The wrist joint actually bends so that the entire foot and wrist, clear up to the stopper pad, are on the ground. So the stopper pad functions just as any other footpad does, but comes into play only at high speed. 🐾

Do cats get hiccups?

YES! CATS, ESPECIALLY KITTENS, commonly get hiccups. Hiccups are sudden spasms of the diaphragm and can be caused by eating too fast and swallowing air, or eating very cold or fatty food. Sometimes the reason just isn't clear.

Trying all the common home remedies for people is pretty useless with cats. Have you ever tried to make a cat breathe into a paper sack or drink from the wrong side of a glass? And if you scared him, I wouldn't blame your cat if he never came out from under the bed. Plus, scaring it doesn't work, either. 🐾

Can cats outrun dogs?

IT DEPENDS. How fat is the cat? How fat is the dog? The fastest house cat, in an open area, cannot outrun the fastest dog.

Nobody knows exactly how fast a cat can run because it's hard to get one to break from a starting box and run around a track. Or to run anywhere you want it to. So you can't exactly time them. And you can't use police radar guns because they don't tend to be very accurate for small objects with rapidly moving parts. But the best estimates place the cat's top speed at about thirty miles per hour—a lot faster than you can run, but a lot slower than a greyhound.

But other factors come into play. How far does the cat have to run? Even if he's being chased by a slightly slower dog, the dog may still catch him if there's no cover nearby. That's because cats are sprinters, and even the sprinters of the dog world are more like marathoners in comparison. This advantage has to do with the muscles in a cat's body. Most of the muscles in a cat's body are made up of anaerobic fibers called "fast twitch" muscles. These muscles give the kitty a burst of speed that enables him to sprint for short distances.

Dogs, on the other hand, possess both anaerobic and aerobic muscles (called "slow twitch" muscles). Such aerobic muscle fiber is the type needed for any sort of endurance running.

So instead of a tortoise and hare situation, we have a kitty and dog situation. If the cat gets too confident and strolls out into an open area, he puts himself in danger, especially if the nearest tree or cover is beyond his sprint range—this is one reason cats instinctively avoid wide-open spaces.

Can cats pull a sled?

NO, AND ANYWAY, WHY would you want them to?

This is one of those funny pictures you might see on the Internet of a team of cats pulling a sled. While it's funny and cute, it really can't happen. Here's why: A cat's body is made up primarily of muscles known as fast-twitch muscles. These muscles do anaerobic types of work (which require a sudden burst of speed). Dogs (especially sled dogs) have both fast-twitch (anaerobic) and slow-twitch (aerobic) muscles that enable them to run with short bursts of speed (anaerobic) but also to go long distances (aerobic). An animal needs those slow-twitch muscles in order to pull a sled for any distance. Hence, physically, cats just can't do it.

But, if that weren't enough, remember that cats aren't team players. The concept of teamwork isn't in a cat's vocabulary.

So, when you're stuck in the frozen Yukon, skip harnessing the cat and look for some sled dogs to get you out of there. 🐾

Can cats swim?

CATS ARE USUALLY WEENIES when it comes to water, but surprisingly, there are cats that do swim. If you look in the wild, tigers are naturally strong swimmers and will pursue their prey through the water.

But what about house cats? Well, there is a breed of cat called the Turkish Van, which will swim. Other cats may swim as well, but it's hit-or-miss as to whether the cat will actually like it. 🐾

Are cats with extra toes weird in other ways?

WITH A CAT, HOW COULD YOU TELL?

Cats (or any animals) with extra toes are called *polydactyls*. There isn't anything unusual about them other than their toes. In human polydactyls, the extra digit is usually on the side of the pinkie, whereas in cats, it's usually on the side of the thumb. Some cats will have even more than one extra toe, sometimes on their front feet, and in others on all four feet (cats normally have five toes on their front feet and four on the rear). The record number of toes is thirty-two (eight on each foot), although some controversy exists over whether this cat may have had a different, unrelated condition in which she actually had double paws on each foot.

In most polydactyls, the extra toes are fully functional, normally jointed, and have a normal retractable claw. No ill effects have been associated with the extra toes. The trait is caused by a single dominant gene, which means that if you want a polydactyl cat, you need to have at least one polydactyl parent.

That's the simple version. It's actually a little more complicated because there are other, less common types of polydactyls that are caused by different, unrelated genes. While the common polydactyl is unrelated to any other anomalies, one trait of "twisty cats" (see the entry in section 10) is often a dewclaw (thumb) with an extra joint, and may be duplicated. These cats would then have an extra toe, but would not be typical polydactyls.

But for your run-of-the-mill polydactyl cat, the only thing different about him is his toes.

Why do cats have wet noses?

CATS HAVE WET NOSES FOR MORE reasons than to jolt you awake on a cold morning. Like most other macrosmatic animals (that is, animals with a very good sense of smell), cats have a rhinarium—that's the technical term for the area of moist, furless skin that we usually refer to as the cat's nose. Researchers believe that the moist surface attracts and dissolves odor molecules, making them more accessible to the cat's sense of smell. 🐾

Are there such things as hypoallergenic cats?

YOU'VE HEARD THE CLAIMS OF some cats being hypoallergenic, that is, able to be tolerated well by allergy sufferers. Maybe you've been looking for such a cat yourself. Are they out there, and can people with allergies tolerate some cats?

Lots of cats have been purported to be hypoallergenic. These include Russian Blues, Cornish Rexes, Sphynx cats, and other breeds. The reality is much more complex. Allergies are tricky things, and while certain cats don't shed as much as others, they still do lose hair. What's more, they can have just as much dander as others cats, which is supposedly the reason why allergy sufferers can't tolerate cats. But wait! Many allergy sufferers aren't allergic to the cat's dander or hair but to the cat's saliva and to sebaceous glands in the cat's skin. So even if you minimize the shedding, it's not the hair but the spit and skin oils.

Awhile back, a company called Allerca claimed to have developed the first genetically modified cat that is hypoallergenic. These cats were supposedly genetically modified to not have the protein that usually causes allergies in people. At this time, it's possible to place an order for a kitten that is supposed to be hypoallergenic. (For more on this, see page 105.) But because allergies are quirky things, a person with allergies can't guarantee what allergens they will react to. Some allergy sufferers are fine with some cats and not with others—even within the same breed. So skip the guesswork and go to the allergist. 🐾

Should you give a cat milk?

WE'VE ALL HEARD OF giving a cat a saucer of milk. It's so prevalent that people do so without giving it a moment's thought. But is this really a good idea?

Actually, no. Most cats are lactose intolerant, meaning that they lack enzymes that allow them to properly digest milk sugar or lactose. So you may be thinking you're doing your kitty a favor when in fact you may be causing gastric upsets.

Our advice is to skip the milk, or at least provide Lactaid or other milk for your cat that has the digestive enzyme already present. 🐾

Are there shedless cats?

IN A WORD, NO. ALL CATS SHED, even the sparsely haired ones like the Cornish Rex or the bald beauties like the Sphynx cat. (The Sphynx actually has a somewhat light fuzz.) While these very short-coated cats shed little, there is no truly "shedless" cat. 🐾

Can cats sunburn?

PASS THE SUNSCREEN, PLEASE, your cat may say. When it comes to sunburn, your cat may be one hot kitty. White cats, cats with white on their faces and ears, cats with pink noses, cats with thin hair in places, and hairless cats can all suffer sunburn.

Sunburn on cats is no fun and can cause nasty sores that won't go away without treatment. And to make matters worse, your cat may develop skin cancer if she insists on getting a tan (or a burn). This is why you should keep your cat inside, away from the sun's harmful rays.

If your cat is fair-nosed or fair-skinned—or especially, hairless!— and is going to spend time in the sun, you need to put sunscreen on her just as you would on yourself. Only beware: She may lick hers off, so make sure it's not toxic. Oh well, at least you can tell your friends you rubbed suntan lotion on a topless girl at the beach. Just leave out the part about the hairy chest.... 🐾

Do hairless cats get cold?

UPON SEEING A HAIRLESS CAT—known as the Sphynx cat—you may start shivering yourself, because the cat looks cold without his fur. Well, you'd be right—they can get cold. If it's cold for you, you can bet it's cold for a Sphynx cat. Even so, Sphynx cats can be pretty clever and choose to cuddle up next to a warm human, another cat, or even (heaven forbid!) a dog. 🐾

Do cats catch colds?

ACHOO! IF YOUR CAT IS SNEEZING and coughing, you might think that she has a cold and that a bowl of chicken soup will make everything better. Well, you're right about one thing: Cats do catch colds. Now, whether chicken soup will fix it is another story.

Cats can have upper respiratory infections usually caused by the feline calicivirus or the feline rhinotracheitis virus (a herpesvirus). These colds are very contagious (to other cats, not humans) and vaccinations are available to prevent them. Some colds can get pretty serious, so, if your kitty is sneezing, it's a good idea to bring her to the vet for treatment. Then, fix her a bowl of warm chicken soup. It won't cure the cold, but maybe she'll start feeling a bit better. 🐾

Why do some cats, like Siamese, have darker points (legs, tail, ears, and face)?

CATS AREN'T THE ONLY SPECIES to have so-called color points, in which the extremities (the face, ears, feet, tail, and in males, the scrotum) are a darker color than the rest of the body. Colored points arise from a mutation that's actually related to albinism; in fact, the genes that cause it are on the same locus as the ones that cause albinos: the C locus. The C gene's job is to make an enzyme called tyrosinase, which is responsible for the first step in making melanin. Various mutations at the C locus mess up this step to varying degrees. While the C allele ("allele" means the alternate form of the gene) is the most dominant, just under that is the C^b allele, which restricts the formation of pigment somewhat and produces a cat that looks brown, like a Burmese. Recessive to the C^b allele is the C^s allele, which is responsible for the color points most associated with the Siamese cat. Finally, most recessive is the c allele, which produces no tyrosinase and so results in an albino.

But back to C^s. The C^s allele (and to a lesser extent, the C^b allele) produces a mutated form of tyrosinase that's heat-sensitive. At normal body temperatures, it hardly works, melanin scarcely develops, and normal coat color isn't expressed. Only in areas of the skin where the temperature is not quite so hot does it function, allowing normal coat color to develop. These cooler areas of the skin are found on the extremities, or points, which is why the darker colors develop only there.

Color-pointed cats tend to get darker in the winter, when the skin gets colder, and paler in the summer, when the skin gets warmer. If you make your pointed cat wear booties, he'll end up with lighter colored feet (as well as a bad attitude). If the hair is clipped, especially on the trunk of the cat, the hair often grows back darker. This is because the skin under the clipped area becomes cooler, so that it acts more like the skin on an extremity, allowing the pigment to form. When that hair is shed, the new hair will come in at its normal lighter color.

Pointed kittens are born white because no such temperature differences exist in the womb. Only as they are exposed to outside temperatures do the extremities develop coloring. 🐾

Why do Siamese cats have blue eyes?

POINTED CATS HAVE BLUE EYES because the iris lacks the pigment of a normal-colored cat. They also lack the pigment in their tapetum, the layer of reflective cells at the back of the eye. That's why these cats will usually have a red eyeshine rather than a green or yellow one. 🐾

What is a fever coat?

NO, IT'S NOT A COAT YOU PUT on your cat to give him a fever. *Fever coat* is the term for a normally dark coat that grows in light after a cat (most often a young cat) has a high fever. The change in color will occur right in the middle of the hair shaft, leaving the hair dark on the tip but light at the root. In a black coat, the hair can turn gray; in a light coat, the coat may be just slightly lighter. It may occur all over the entire body or affect only the ruff and pantaloons. The extremities, because they stay cooler, also tend to stay the normal, darker color. In pointed cats, it may appear simply as spectacles around the eyes. Don't worry—it will grow back to its normal color as soon as the hair is shed! 🐾

Why do cats get hair balls?

"HACK! HACK! HACK!" You know what's coming next. A big, slimy old goober of a hair ball. But why do cats get these icky things?

Well, if you hadn't noticed, cats do an extraordinary amount of grooming. That means that the cat hair has to go somewhere, usually down the gullet. Because of that, the hair often collects in the stomach, even though some passes through. Since all the hair isn't passing through, the only place for it to go is right back up—and usually into your shoes you were going to wear to work. Lovely. 🐾

Do old cats get gray hair?

IT'S TOUGH GETTING OLD—and one of the first signs is graying hair. You may wonder whether cats get gray hair as well.

Well, yes, although some cats, like some people, don't show gray as well. The cats with dark-colored hair show gray more readily, starting at the chin and muzzle. Some will show gray on the paws and eventually all over the head.

It's a good thing cats aren't as vain as we are—there isn't a lot of kitty hair coloring out there. 🐾

Why do black cats often have a reddish tinge to their coat?

YOUR NORMALLY JET BLACK CAT suddenly doesn't look so black anymore. Is he just trying to make himself a luckier omen? Or is something else amiss? It turns out that several dietary factors can deblacken a black coat.

Diets with too much zinc, too little copper, or, most often, too little tyrosine can all cause loss of hair color. These ingredients all interact with or otherwise affect the production of tyrosinase (see "Why do some cats, like Siamese, have darker points," above). It's an enzyme responsible for making melanin, the major pigment in cat hair.

The amount of tyrosine recommended in cat foods to keep kittens and cats healthy is 4.5 grams plus 12 grams of phenylalanine per kilogram of amino acids. Don't worry about getting this exact; you're probably not going to be measuring this out in your kitchen.

However, the problem is, if you feed black cats these quantities, they develop reddish brown coats, probably because the tyrosinase levels aren't high enough to produce the melanin needed for dark black pigment. If you raise the levels to 18 grams of tyrosine per kilogram, the coats will grow back in nice and black.

Tyrosine is found in meat, eggs, and dairy products, so if your cat is otherwise healthy, adding a little more of these foods to his diet may blacken his coat. But always check with your veterinarian first, since such supplementation can be harmful to cats with some other health problems. In addition, some coat changes can be caused by health problems, such as a hypoactive thyroid. 🐾

Do cats pant like dogs?

CATS CAN PANT, BUT UNLIKE DOGS, they don't do it just because of hot weather. When a cat pants, it's most often because he's very stressed. If he pants from heat, it's usually only when he's extremely hot, which means you should take measures to cool him immediately.

Cats evolved as desert animals, so they seem to be able to cope with heat better than dogs. Their large, thin ears allow the blood flowing through them to cool, an important mechanism in many hot climate species. They don't have sweat glands like we do, except on their paw pads, but the paws can't sweat enough to really cool the cat. Cats also groom themselves more often in hot weather, depositing saliva on their fur, which then cools them slightly as it evaporates. They will also seek shade and cool surfaces, such as in sinks or on tile, to spread themselves out on.

You can help a long-haired cat stay cool by clipping his fur shorter—not right to the skin, which makes it prone to sunburn, but so that the cat is wearing a shirt of fur rather than an overcoat. If you don't want to sacrifice that luxurious cape, you can just clip the tummy area, which you won't notice. But he will, and he'll thank you for it! For any cat, you can help out in the fur-wetting department. No, not by licking his hair for him! Just wet your hands or a paper towel and then his fur, or stand him up in some shallow water. He may act perturbed, but deep down he likes it. After all, a cat's got to keep his cool.

Does a Manx have less balance because he doesn't have a tail?

ALTHOUGH A NORMAL CAT that suddenly loses its tail may at first have some problems with balance, it adjusts quickly and soon regains its sense of balance. Or at least, it seems to. Researchers who have carefully studied the cat's ability to walk across a narrow beam, and stay on it when it moved, have found that the cats use their tail to realign their hips over the beam. But when cats had no ability to move their tail, they couldn't adjust as well and tended to fall off the beam more often. Manx cats weren't included in the study; Manx owners say their cats never appear to have any problems with balance, despite their lack of a tail. So at least in daily life, the lack of a tail doesn't seem to affect them. However, it would be interesting to really put them to the test with a more challenging balancing act. 🐾

Can cats be right-pawed or left-pawed?

LIKE LEFT-HANDED PEOPLE, some cats are called "southpaws," but do they really show a preference for their left paw? It turns out that many cats do show a paw preference; in one recent study in which cats had to use their paw to reach for food, 46 percent preferred to use their right paw, 44 percent preferred their left paw, and 10 percent used both equally. About 60 percent of the cats used one paw 100 percent of the time. And it wasn't just a passing fancy: the preferences were stable over a ten-week testing period. In another study, cats tended to prefer their left paw to try to grab a moving object.

You can test your own cat's paw preference in a variety of ways. Place a tantalizing toy or treat just out of reach under a barrier, and see which paw he uses to reach for it. Place his food in a bowl that's too narrow for his face to fit in, and see which paw he uses to fish it out. Or stick a piece of tape on his head or nose and see which paw he uses to pull it off. 🐾

Do wet cats shake themselves dry like wet dogs do?

MANY SPECIES OF ANIMALS will shake off like a dog after getting their body wet. Cats do this as well, but not quite as vigorously as dogs. But they are masters at shaking off each foot individually. Dogs don't do that. Then cats use their tongue to lick as much moisture from their coat as possible. That's a tough job. Go on, go get a towel and help! 🐾

Do cats get boogers?

YOU NEVER SEE A CAT PICKING HIS NOSE. Is it because they're discreet? Or is it just because they'd put a hole in their nose with those sharp claws?

Cats do get nasal discharge, even the, um, solid kind, more so than dogs, but less than people. They tend to either lick or sneeze away the offending substance, however. A cat with persistently thick or greenish or reddish discharge, however, should be checked by a veterinarian for a possible infection or growth. Or be taught to use a tissue. 🐾

Are lilies poisonous to cats?

IT'S SPRINGTIME AND YOU'VE JUST purchased beautiful Easter lilies, but a friend warns you that if your cat eats them, your cat could be pushing up daisies. Are lilies dangerous to cats?

Absolutely! Lilies have been known to cause renal damage and even death in cats. So while they're safe for dogs, they're fatal to cats. You can skip the flowers this year. 🐾

Do cats get gas?

IN A STUDY OF PET AND PEOPLE GAS, it was reported that odorless gases (nitrogen, oxygen, hydrogen, carbon dioxide, and methane) make up 99 percent of all intestinal gas. Yeah, right. I guess it's that other 1 percent that can be deadly. That percent is made up of volatile sulfur compounds.

Gas can be caused by swallowing air (a major component, but more so in dogs than cats). It can also be caused by bacterial fermentation in the large colon of foods that contain a lot of fiber or poorly digestible protein or foods that contain large amounts of indigestible sugars. Such foods include soybeans and foods containing fructose, resistant starches, or fermentable fiber. Lactose-containing foods such as milk or milk products are also major offenders.

If you have a stinky kitty, make sure he's not gulping his food, and try to feed him high-quality proteins and avoid soy-based foods. Also avoid milk products or sugary foods. Increase your cat's exercise; at least he might have his gas attack somewhere other than in your lap. If your cat has a lot of gas, he may suffer from inflammatory bowel disease or some other problem that merits a visit to the vet.

At least cats are small, and their cat farts proportionately so. That may be scant comfort when his butt is five inches from your face on your pillow, however. 🐾

Is the cat's purr a natural thing?

IT LOOKS LIKE IT MUST BE. Purring takes energy, yet cats seem to purr not only when they are content, but especially when they are injured or ill. And when a cat is ill, it doesn't make sense for it to expend energy purring. Some behaviorists simply say they do it to calm themselves—perhaps at a time when self-licking would be too strenuous an activity. But that still doesn't adequately explain why species from lions to house cats would purr when injured.

One explanation, however, may have to do with the healing power of low-frequency sound. In people, vibrational stimulation from certain frequencies serves to relieve suffering in 82 percent of persons suffering from acute and chronic pain. It also encourages new tissue and bone growth, aids tendon and muscle repair, improves local circulation and oxygenation, and reduces swelling. Cats are famous for their ability to heal after surgery or injury, surpassing not only people, but dogs. Could there be a link?

Scientists did studies measuring cat purrs to see if they matched up with healing frequencies. In both big and little cat species, purr frequencies fell within the range of the best therapeutic vibrational frequencies. Kitty, heal thyself! No, don't get any money-saving ideas—your cat still needs to go to the vet if he gets hurt.

Purring, however, may have an evolutionary reason beyond healing. Cats, like most predators, spend the majority of their time sleeping. If a person spent that much time in bed, he or she would experience muscle atrophy and bone density loss. In fact, that's a problem for astronauts, even considering the relatively short time they spend weightless. So how does a lazy cat stay so fit? Some scientists think the purr may be responsible. Purring may be a low-energy way to stimulate bones and muscles. So the next time you see your cat lounging about purring, don't bother him. He's really hard at work. 🐾

How do cats purr?

THROUGH THE YEARS, scientists have come up with all sorts of theories to explain how cats purr. At one time it was thought they had a special purring organ, but it turns out they don't. Another theory was that they had a special patch of soft tissue in the neck or diaphragm that vibrated, but nobody has ever found one. Yet another theory is that purring is caused by the vibrations of a series of small bones connecting the skull and larynx called the hyoid apparatus, but no evidence has supported it. Yet another is that purring is the result of blood hitting the aorta. Again, a great theory, except that there's no evidence for it.

The best accepted theory is that purring is an involuntary reflex caused by neural impulses, which in turn cause the muscles in the larynx and diaphragm to relax and constrict rhythmically about twenty-five times per second or more. This causes pressure changes in the windpipe that are then superimposed on normal breathing. Purring occurs during both inhalation and exhalation.

It's still just a theory, though. It's hard to get a cat to hold still and purr while you stick a probe down his throat. And anesthetized cats don't purr. But really, what would you expect? Cats have to keep some of their secrets, or they wouldn't be mysterious. 🐾

How does a cat retract its claws?

CATS DON'T, TECHNICALLY, retract their claws. The cat's claws are in a relaxed state when they are recessed, so it's more correct to say that cats unsheathe their claws when they want to use them. They do this by calling on certain muscles that cause the bottom of the claw bed to retract, pulling the claw down and forward. When that muscle relaxes, the claw is released and springs back up inside its sheath. 🐾

Why can't a cheetah retract its claws?

UNLIKE MOST CATS, the cheetah's relaxed claw is still exposed. It's not so much that he can't retract it (see previous question), or even that it's in such a different position than other cats' relaxed toes, but the sheath simply doesn't cover it to the extent it does in other species.

By the way, the cheetah isn't the only cat that doesn't retract its claws. The flat-headed cat and the fishing cat, both of Southeast Asia, as well as Geoffrey's cat, from South America, also cannot fully retract their claws. 🐾

Do cats get wrinkles when they age?

HOW WOULD YOU TELL BENEATH all that fur? That's why we went to the hairless Sphynx for the answer. Cat skin does lose much of its elasticity as a cat ages, but instead of wrinkling, it tends to sag a bit. But overall, cats aren't plagued by wrinkling in old age. So fear not—no need for antiwrinkle creams or Botox to keep your kitty looking youthful! 🐾

Do cats get goose bumps?

AGAIN, HOW WOULD YOU KNOW? And again, we turned to hairless cats for the answer. Cats don't appear to get goose bumps in cold weather, even though they do puff out their coats somewhat for better insulation in frigid climates. And instead of goose bumps appearing beneath their hair when they fuzz their tail, you really can't see anything except a slight wrinkling of the skin in places. 🐾

Do cats ever bite their own tongue?

CATS HAVE EITHER MORE SENSE or more coordination than the average person, because they don't seem to bite their tongue. Then again, they seldom try to talk with their mouth full, either. Still, do you think a cat would ever actually admit to biting its tongue if it did? How uncool. 🐾

Can you tickle a cat?

IF YOU TRY TO TICKLE A CAT in his armpits, he's more likely to scratch you and run off in a huff than he is to fall down helplessly laughing.

You can't tickle a cat like you can tickle a person. But you can tickle a cat on the bottom of its footpads, or between them. He still won't laugh, but he'll jerk his foot away over and over. Then he'll stalk away, muttering in kitty language about stupid human pastimes. 🐾

Why do tomcats have big jowls?

YOU CAN TELL A MATURE INTACT male cat from a distance just by looking at his face. Tomcats have very large jaw muscles compared with female cats or neutered male cats. The jowls are the result of testosterone acting on the muscles, making the tom particularly buff in the face. Nobody knows why it seems to affect the jaw muscles more in cats than in other species, but it likely has to do with the fact that during breeding, the tom grabs the female by the nape of her neck with his jaws. Stronger jaws mean she's less likely to squirm away, or twist around and smack him. Plus, maybe cats think it looks macho. 🐾

Why does tomcat urine smell so strong?

THE SHORT ANSWER IS, I guess they want to advertise their manliness. But if you've ever been around a place where an intact male cat has sprayed, you know we're talking industrial strength urine here. What's he got in it?

In fact, the urine marking of tomcats doesn't just smell stronger, it *is* stronger. Cat urine has a fatty component that enables it to cling to surfaces. At one time, scientists thought this component came from anal sac secretions, but they proved it didn't by inserting a dye into male lion anal sacs (I wonder how much that guy got paid!) and then checking the urine for dye. It wasn't there.

Instead, it probably comes from the kidney. In fact, levels of urinary lipids in general correlate with kidney fat reserves, which in turn correlate with good health, so the amount of lipids in a scent mark could be a way for the tom to advertise how healthy he is. More likely, though, the lipids are important because they retard the release of volatile compounds, which basically means they act as a time-release mechanism for the smelly parts of the urine. Oh boy.

But that still doesn't explain why tom urine is so pungent. It appears to be simply a matter of testosterone and its metabolic products in the urine. The only solution is to castrate him. Or get a set of nose plugs. 🐾

Can cats cry real tears?

CATS CAN CERTAINLY PRODUCE TEARS, but don't do it in response to emotions; rather, they react to eye irritations, allergies, or even clogged tear ducts. If your cat is tearing, take him to the veterinarian, not to the grief counselor. 🐾

2

Q CAT
BEHAVIOR A

Why do cats bury their poop?

IF YOU'VE HAD NOTHING to do all day and are bored enough, you might notice that your cat buries his poop after he visits the litter box. Why does he do that? And why do some cats not do that?

Cats bury poop in the wild not because they're particularly fastidious, but rather because they want to keep themselves hidden from other predators and from more dominant cats. These wildcats know that a good way to keep alive is to be out of sight and out of mind.

Some cats, however, don't cover their poop. These cats are very confident kitties that figure out they're top cat. Either that, or it's time to clean out the litter box, big time! 🐾

Why do cats purr when you pet them?

YOU'VE NO DOUBT HEARD that rumbling sound your cat makes—a vibrating low thrum that seems to tell you the cat is happy and contented. But, as explained earlier, cats purr for a variety of reasons: when they're happy and when they're sick or injured. They even purr when they're giving birth, are nervous or afraid, and when they're dying. So, while we know that cats purr when they are happy, we don't really understand why they purr in the first place.

Many behaviorists think that cats may purr voluntarily to comfort themselves. A fearful or sick cat's purr may be a way to tell herself that everything will be all right and to calm down when things are scary or painful. A purr may also mean, "I need some petting to help me feel better" when she's just not feeling that great. At the same time, a purring cat could be saying, "I'm really so happy to have a friend like you." Confusing, isn't it?

Scientists are in much the same boat, unable to explain to this day how a cat purrs, except that it seems to have something to do with breathing and the cat's voice box. The exact mechanism remains a mystery.

But there's no mystery when your cat sits in your lap and purrs away, is there? 🐾

Why do cats sleep on top of your head (or crushing some other body part) in bed?

YOU GO TO BED AT NIGHT, and in the morning you wake up with your cat on top of your head. Or maybe the cat is making your legs numb, or you feel a crushing weight on your chest. You're beginning to think that those old wives tales about cats sucking out one's breath might be true. What's going on here?

Cats love warmth, and believe it or not, you're a great big hot water bottle or self-generating heating pad. People lose a lot of heat from the top of their heads, and your cat can sense this, so she lies where it's warm and cozy.

If your cat doesn't lie on your head, perhaps it's because another area might be more comfy. And here you thought she loved you! 🐾

Why do cats always want to see what's behind a door?

YOU CLOSE A DOOR, AND THE moment you do, the cat is there yowling to have the door open. The door could be open a thousand times a day, but now that you've closed it, your cat is annoyed and wants to go through. Why?

Well, doors are the bane of all cats—just ask them. There isn't a cat out there who thinks a closed door is OK. Mostly because they want to know what is behind that door you're keeping them from, but also because they figure it's part of their territory, and you're blocking it off. At least, that's how they look at it.

You've heard of curiosity killing the cat? Well, there you go. 🐾

Why do cats like to shred paper and cardboard?

YOU HAVE A CARDBOARD BOX FULL of stuff, and your cat goes right over to it and starts shredding it with her claws. What gives?

Well, look at the box like your cat would. It has enough resistance to withstand a really good scratch and makes a satisfying noise when scratched. What's more, it's probably in an ideal place for scratching, namely, where she'd scratch if you had been thoughtful enough to put out a scratching post.

What your cat is telling you is to give her some more scratchers of different materials and to station them throughout the house. In fact, many wonderful scratchers are made from cardboard or paper, which will satisfy her scratching urge.

Why do cats dig in planters?

YOU BRING HOME A LOVELY potted plant and, before you know it, your cat is digging like the Army Corps of Engineers, destroying your plant and throwing dirt everywhere. Why?

Well, there are several reasons for this. The first is that dirt feels wonderful to a cat's paws and, because it's a natural instinct to dig in dirt and poop, your cat finds that oh so enticing. Then, there's the need for a good scratch. What better way to make his presence known than by scratching up a perfectly good plant?

The way to stop this is to put two-sided tape across the planter and have your greenery in a big enough planter so that your cat can't reach it. Or, better yet, keep the plants away from your cat.

Why do cats seek out the one person in the room who doesn't like them?

YOU KNOW THE STORY: A group of people visit a friend's house and the cat disappears. One of the people announces he hates cats. Before you know it, the cat is sitting in that person's lap. What's up with that? Is the cat psychic and therefore has figured out which person hates it? Well, maybe, but it more likely has to do with the signals that person is sending out.

You see, cats get nervous about being in the spotlight. That's why when strangers come into a house, some cats will naturally skedaddle until they feel comfortable enough around the people to come out. When they do come out, they're not necessarily looking for too much attention. Instead, they're looking to feel safe. Oddly enough, the person who ignores the cat the most is the person who seems the least intimidating. That person isn't giving the cat what can be perceived as threatening signals: eye contact, approaching movements, etc. In fact, the person is acting coolly neutral. That's what the cat likes.

So, if you really don't like cats and have become a cat magnet, change your behavior. Look at the cat. Try to pet it. While you may not make the cat go away, you might start liking cats more. 🐾

Why do cats knead with their paws?

YOU'RE SPENDING SOME QUALITY TIME with your kitty. She's lying down in your lap and purring mightily, when suddenly she starts moving her paws back and forth in a rhythmic motion, like she's kneading bread. Her sharp claws may go into your leg and come out in a quick motion. Not enough to scratch, but enough to feel as though you have needles prickling you. What's going on?

As you may have guessed, kneading is one of the greatest compliments your cat can pay you. Your cat is telling you that she trusts you and feels happy and secure around you. You see, she used to do this when she was with her mom—and when she does this, she's telling you that you're just like a big mom to her. Pretty cool, huh? 🐾

Do cats talk when they meow?

MEOW, MEOW, MEOW. You've probably heard cats meow when they want something, but you may be wondering if meowing is a form of speech.

Well, yes and no. You may be surprised to learn that most wild and feral cats don't meow that much—and certainly not to each other. Meowing, it seems, is a cat's way of getting our attention.

Some cats are naturally mouthy. Oriental breeds, such as Siamese, are naturally chatty cats. When dealing with people, cats make what we react to best—verbal sounds. Our reaction to their meows causes them to meow more. So, when a cat is meowing loudly at her food bowl, she's calling you to come feed her. Makes sense, doesn't it?

But is it a form of speech? Not really. Cats have various vocalizations that mean things such as "Hey, I'm hungry," "This is scary," or "I'm looking for a mate," but they don't have meows that signify words.

Why do cats rub up against you?

YOU'VE PROBABLY EXPERIENCED THIS quite a bit if you have cats or if you know someone who does. The cat comes over and rubs her head and face against you or maybe rubs up against your legs. What does that mean?

You probably won't be surprised if I tell you it's a sign of affection. Cats rub against people because they like them, and also to claim them. You see, cats have special sebaceous glands in the cheeks, mouth, and chin that secrete a special hormone that identifies you with the cat's scent (we can't smell them, but a cat can). When a cat rubs against you, she is marking you as a special human and laying claim to you, just in case any strange cats might be present.

Likewise, cats will rub up against objects around the house in order to harmlessly mark the objects as part of their territory. It reminds the cat of where her boundaries are and also lets any stray animals know what is going on. 🐾

Why do cats sometimes bite a person who is petting them?

A CAT MAY COME UP TO YOU for petting or affection, and while petting, the cat whaps you with her claws or bites you hard. You're left scared and the cat goes off angry. Why this sudden outburst?

This is a common reaction to *overstimulation*, that is, the cat becomes riled up because there's too much petting.

The problem is that the cat doesn't want to be petted or held for long periods of time. This isn't necessarily her problem, per se, it's yours. The cat may be able to tolerate only a few rubs, or maybe not even that. But if the cat hops into your lap or approaches nearby and brushes up against you, you can pet her (provided this isn't a strange cat). Just watch carefully for the signs.

Signs that she is becoming overstimulated include flattening ears, dilating pupils, stiffening up, fur moving like a shiver throughout her body, tail lashing back and forth and, of course, a low growl. If a cat shows any of these signs, stop petting her. If necessary, move her off your lap. The idea is to react to these signs first so that the cat doesn't feel the need to demonstrate her displeasure. She's trying to give you the signals that say "Hey, stop petting me!" before she has to do something about it. 🐾

Why is herding cats like, well, herding cats?

YOU'VE NO DOUBT HEARD the phrase "herding cats," which describes a near impossibility of getting people to do the same thing at once. However, you may be wondering why doing anything with cats is, well, like herding cats.

Cats are independent by nature and have found this to be an incredibly successful strategy for hundreds of thousands of years. Because our feline friends don't hunt in packs—and don't usually interact a lot with members of their species (they enjoy their privacy)—the concept of doing anything for the team is foreign to them. After all, there's no "team" in "I."

So, the domestic cat is all for me and me for me. Which suits him just fine. Which is why you won't see too many cats engaging in team sports. 🐾

Why do cats bring things they've caught or found to you?

IF YOU'VE EVER BEEN BLESSED by dead rodents or pieces of dead rodents brought in by a cat, you may say "ugh." After all, it's pretty disgusting having a mouse head left on your doorstep. But let's look at it from a cat's perspective.

Cats are hunters and true carnivores, meaning they can't live without meat. Cats need an amino acid called taurine, which they get only by eating meat. Their bodies don't manufacture taurine, so they must get it from an outside source. Plants do not provide taurine, hence the need to eat flesh products.

Cats hunt because it is their very nature to do so. When a cat brings you a mouse or part of a mouse, she's sharing the hunt with you. Indeed, she may be training you to hunt, since it appears you're incapable of it.

When cats don't have animals to hunt, sometimes they'll leave bits of food from their plate or even a toy mouse for you. Thank her profusely. After all, she's deemed you worthy to share her meal. 🐾

How do cats learn to use kitty litter?

YOU BRING A PUPPY HOME and part of his training is learning to go outside. You bring a kitten home and—look at that, he uses the litter box. But why?

Cats instinctively know to poop and pee in something soft like fine dirt or sand. Showing your kitten the box is all that is usually required to litter-box train a cat. How cool is that? 🐾

Why do some cats lick people?

WHAT DO YOU HAVE ON YOUR HAND? Seriously.

Actually, cats will lick people and even lightly bite their noses as a sign of affection. Other signs of affection include head butts, touching nose to nose, and looking into your eyes.

Well, there's no accounting for taste. 🐾

Why do cats jump up on people's laps?

YOU'VE SEEN IT BEFORE. You sit down in your good clothes, and the cat is all over you, jumping up into your lap. Now you have cat fur all over. Ugh. Why do they do this?

Actually, this is quite normal behavior. If the cat is naturally affectionate or curious, she is probably going to go where the action is, namely towards you. The fact that you have your good clothes on doesn't matter one bit to her. In fact, it is probably the case that the more agitated or annoyed you act, the more you pique your cat's curiosity. (Plus, you probably smell more interesting in the new clothes.)

Cats will jump into people's laps as a way of getting their attention, as a sign they may want to be petted, or because humans are warm there and the cats want a live hot water bottle. 🐾

How do cats know it's time for dinner?

CATS CAN'T TELL TIME, but they have an uncanny ability for harassing you if you're just a few minutes late serving their supper.

Oh, who am I kidding? They'll try to convince you it's suppertime twenty-four hours a day.

But truly, they do know when it's time to eat, and it's not just that they're hungry because they haven't been fed yet. All animals, including people, seem to have a gut feeling—literally—for when it's time to eat. The gut actually begins to contract and gets ready to rumble right before the time it's used to getting food, and does so regardless of whether the cat had a previous snack.

Just as we, and cats, have a circadian rhythm that controls our sleep-wake cycle, they have a gut rhythm that tells them it's time—or past time—to eat. Of course, for most cats, that rhythm seems to be pretty much going full blast all day long. 🐾

Why do cats walk across computer keyboards?

YOU'RE WORKING ON SOMETHING very important when suddenly—akjsferilt;gh'rr—your cat walks across your keyboard. You shoo her away. She hits the delete key. You push her off; she reformats your hard drive. What's up with that?

Actually, your cat is very concerned that this clicky-sounding thing you tap on could be taking away your attention from her so completely. So she comes to investigate and distract. After all, she's read the news that too much computer time isn't good for you. 🐾

Why do cats play with toys beneath doors or around corners?

CATS LOVE TO PLAY WITH TOYS, but what really gets Maggie's cat going is when you give her toys she can bat beneath doors or play with around corners. A boring game becomes exciting when the toy is hidden just beyond her cat's view.

It's not just Maggie's cat either. Most cats love the thrill of the chase beneath doors and around corners. Why?

Well, part of it is instinctual. Hidden prey actually piques a cat's interest. But why focus around corners and under doors?

A cat expert friend of Maggie's suggested that when cats hunt larger prey, such as rats, they often try to shield themselves to avoid getting bitten by the prey and thereby injured. So by working the "prey" (whether they're toys or real) around a corner and batting at it, the cat is wearing the critter out safely so she can administer the death bite. And you thought it was all in fun. 🐾

Why do cats play at night?

BECAUSE THEY SLEEP ALL DAY.

Seriously, cats are nocturnal hunters, and that's why they are more active at night. Or maybe they just like the Late Night Show. 🐾

Why do cats chatter when stalking?

YOUR CAT SEES A BIRD OUTSIDE the window and starts stalking it and making a chattering noise at the same time. Why does he do that?

Your cat isn't dumb. He knows that he can't get to the bird and is frustrated that he can't, so he makes a frustrated or excited chatter when he sees the bird. He'll also make this sound if the prey escapes—muttering to himself.

And you thought he was talking to the birds! 🐾

Why do cats swish or lash their tail?

YOU KNOW THAT WHEN DOGS WAG THEIR TAIL, it can mean they're happy, but what about when cats do it? And why do they swish or lash their tail?

Cats use their tails for communication, just as dogs do. When a cat swishes her tail from side to side fast, it can be a real sign of trouble: Namely, the cat is agitated and wants to be left alone. But the tail swish can also indicate that the cat is hunting and is excited. Some cats will stand still, but their tail will be moving, hoping to cause agitation in their prey so they can see and jump them. A slow tail swish may mean the cat is happy and contented.

But what about a twitch or flick of the tail? Like people, cats can be indecisive as to what they want to do and will twitch their tail. Tail twitching can convey irritation, pensiveness, or even a response when you call your cat's name while she's sleeping. Some cats will hear their name and respond with a tail flick, saying in essence, "Yeah, I heard you, but you're not as important as my nap."

Isn't that the truth?

Why do cats arch their back?

WHEN WE TALK ABOUT CATS arching their back, it usually has to do with the Halloween-type cat posture. And while it looks scary for us, that's not the entire story—it's scary for them too.

Cats arch their back to look bigger than they are in the face of something that scares them. Like dogs, their hair stands on end due to piloerection (the same thing that causes raised hackles in dogs and goose bumps in humans). So, if you see a puffed-out cat with an arched back, chances are she's seen something pretty scary.

Or maybe she saw your new outfit.

Why do cats get stuck in trees?

IT'S A CLICHÉ, REALLY: The cat that ends up in the tree to be rescued by the fire department. But do cats get stuck in trees? And if so, why?

Cats are great climbers, but only up, not down. This is because the shape of their claws makes it easy for them to hoist themselves up and hang on. Because they'd rather go head-first down, and their claws won't hold them (not being able to grip upside down), they get a bit flummoxed over how to get down. When they finally figure out that they need to go backwards the way they came, it's no big deal, but it takes a bit of figuring out, and some cats don't get it at all.

So, how do you get a cat out of a tree? Ladder, we're thinking. Only don't fall. 🐾

Why does the cat tease the dog?

YOU'VE SEEN CATS SIT ON TOP OF FENCES, tantalizingly close to the dogs beneath them and calmly grooming themselves while the dogs bark. "There's that cat teasing the dogs again," you think.

But do cats tease dogs? Well, that's open for interpretation.

You see, the dog's barking and lunging isn't really on the cat's radar screen. The cat knows he's safe and is not really interested in what the dog is doing. As far as the cat is concerned, the dog is just something noisy and annoying. So, he might as well continue to groom himself and think about something else.

We call it teasing; the cat calls it ignoring. 🐾

Why do cats eat dog food?

YOU LEAVE THE DOG'S FOOD OUT, and sure enough, here comes the cat over to the dish and starts eating it. What have we here? Doesn't he know he's not supposed to eat from it?

Actually, no. Your cat sees a bowl that the dog eats out of, and while it's dreadfully inconvenient for that noisy critter to be eating out of the bowl, the cat figures it's his too. After all, it's all in the cat's territory and it's food in a bowl, left out for animals.

But dog food doesn't have the right nutrients for a cat, which is why you just can't let your cat eat the dog's food. Pick up the dog's food after each of his meals and feed your cat separately. 🐾

Why do cats scratch on things?

SCRATCHING IS SOMETHING EVERY cat does. It's as natural to them as breathing or eating. Cats scratch for a variety of reasons. They do it to mark their territory, that is, to let other cats know that they're around. They do it to file down their claws and keep them sharp for hunting. They do it for exercise and stretching. And they do it because they like to.

Because scratching is very important to a cat—it's how they communicate—taking away their ability to scratch leaves a maimed and unhappy cat. Many behavior problems result from declawing cats, which is why you should never declaw except under the most extreme circumstances, such as if you are immune-compromised due to HIV/AIDS, cancer, or an organ transplant. 🐾

Why do cats sleep so much?

WHAT ELSE DO THEY HAVE TO DO? I mean, really; with a schedule of eat, groom, scratch, chase a toy...what else is there for cats to do but sleep?

OK, well, as predators, cats tend to sleep about sixteen hours a day. This is just normal, and sleeping that long seems to be right for them. They're nocturnal hunters, which explains why they sleep so much during the day. However, why they sleep so much still leaves experts scratching their heads.

Maybe our cats just find us boring. 🐾

Why are cats such picky eaters?

WHEN COMPARED WITH DOGS, which will eat darn near anything, including rocks and their own poop, cats seem downright picky. So why do cats turn up their noses at certain foods?

It may have to do with freshness. Cats don't like spoiled or rancid food. It affects their sensibilities. So if something smells wrong to them, they turn up their noses at it.

Of course, if your cat isn't eating at all, that may be a sign of a more serious problem. That's something to talk to your vet about.

Why do cats groom themselves constantly?

YOU SEE CATS GROOMING themselves all the time. Usually it's pretty methodical, and they'll even groom their faces by licking their paw and wiping it across their face. But why do they do it?

In a word, it's instinctual. Mom cats start it right from the get-go with their kittens, so being clean is something that stays with cats their entire lives. What's more, cats will often groom each other as a form of social bonding among littermates and housemates (if they like each other).

Plus, who likes a dirty cat?

Why do some cats suck wool?

IT ALL STARTS QUITE INNOCUOUSLY. You notice a sock with a hole here or there. Then, you notice that a blanket is wet or has a few holes. Then, something else more important gets ruined. Maybe it's a special sweater. Maybe it's some laundry you just washed. You know your cat is chewing and sucking on the clothing (especially wool) but you don't know why.

No one knows the actual reason why cats suck wool (and eat clothing), but there are various theories. One thought is that cats that are taken away from their mother too soon are prone to do this. Another reason suggests that cats that suck wool need fiber in their diets.

If you have a wool sucker, you probably are going to have to keep your clothing away from your cat, plus provide him a diet high in fiber. A cat behaviorist can help you out with that. 🐾

Why don't cats like their tummies rubbed like dogs?

YOU MAY SEE A CAT WITH HER BELLY fur exposed, but the moment you try to pet her there, she's all claws and teeth. Why this reaction? Doesn't she want her tummy rubbed like Fido?

The short answer is no, with a capital N-O! Cats and dogs have different styles of communicating. You rub a dog there and he's your buddy. You rub a cat there, and you've violated your cat's trust.

Most cats roll over for one of two reasons. The first is that the cat is relaxed with you enough to show her belly. It's not an invitation for a pet, in most circumstances. It's saying, "I trust you enough to leave myself open to you: Don't abuse it."

The second reason is that the belly up actually can be a defensive posture. If you try to get at the cat's belly, you have four weapons to get around, namely, those four sets of sharp claws. A cat that is really angered will bite and hold with her teeth while she rakes those sharp claws down whatever she perceives is attacking her. If it's your arm, it's no great loss, in her opinion. 🐾

Can cats and dogs get along?

YOU'VE PROBABLY HEARD THE ADAGE "fighting like cats and dogs." You've probably seen a dog chase a cat. There are often cat and dog owners. But will the twain ever meet?

According to the Pet Products Manufacturers Association, a full 45 percent of households own more than one pet, and 46 percent of dog owners own cats as well. That's a huge number, if you look at it. Certainly, dogs and cats can and do get along.

But don't take my word for it—check out your pet-owning friends who have cats and dogs. That alone should tell you that "fighting like cats and dogs" doesn't always happen, or does it? 🐾

Do cats bury things like dogs do?

YES, THEY DO. CATS WILL BURY POOP to hide from other predators. Cats will also bury food to eat again at another time. It's very similar to wildcats burying their kills in order to come back and eat them later on. 🐾

Are yawns contagious to cats?

ABSOLUTELY! TRY IT SOMETIME while your cat is looking. Yawn at your cat and watch him yawn. Something psychological about watching someone yawn causes us to yawn, be it human or cat.

Yawning is contagious to cats, just as it is to people. Of course, you just might seem boring, and your cat is trying to tell you something. 🐾

Can cats get amnesia?

HOW WOULD YOU TELL? Maybe he suddenly wouldn't respond to his name or sit when you told him? Like I said, how would you tell the difference?

When people have a severe accident, especially one leading to loss of consciousness, they often get what's called *retrograde amnesia*. That means they may lose their memory of events leading up to their loss of consciousness, perhaps those of only the last few minutes, but sometimes those of the previous week. But it's not like it is in the soaps, where they forget who they are and end up joining the Mob.

It's quite possible that cats suffer from a similar loss of memory regarding events that occurred right before a serious accident, but there's no way for us to know that. On the other hand, maybe that's why some cats that survive after getting hit by cars wander out in front of the next one as soon as they get off their crutches. 🐾

Why do some cats not like to eat out of their food dish?

IT'S NOT THAT THEY'RE PICKY, IT'S JUST that you didn't bring out the good china.

Many cats dislike their food bowls largely because they're uncomfortable for them to eat from. Cats, having wide faces and even wider whiskers, dislike eating out of standard bowls because the sides of the bowls irritate their sensitive whiskers.

But that's not all: Some cats dislike their bowls because they are plastic, which is porous and can harbor germs, thus making the bowl smell "wrong" to them.

The best bowl is a wide china or stainless steel one with low sides that can be washed frequently. Your cat will purr over your good taste in tableware. 🐾

Why do cats sniff butts?

YOUR CAT MEETS A NEW CAT ON A STROLL, and what's the first thing he does? He kind of sidles around to it and tries for a butt sniff while the other cat does the same. And why shouldn't he? The area around the anus has glands that secrete all sorts of personal information about him. We don't know exactly what, but it probably gives hints about his sexual status, perhaps even his social dominance. All we do know is that it's the feline equivalent of checking out a fellow conventioneer's badge that says, "Hi, I'm Fluffy." 🐾

Why do cats pee outside the litter box?

YOUR CAT IS LITTER-BOX TRAINED, or so you think. Then, one day you smell something awful where you shouldn't. What's up with that?

Well, there are several reasons why a cat might choose not to use her litter box. The first reason is medical. Most cats figure that if they hurt when they pee or poop, it must be the litter box (they have no concept of something within them causing pain) and therefore they avoid it. So, urinary tract infections and other ailments can cause your cat to think "outside the box."

Then, there's the insecurity issue. If you have a lot of new things going on: new people, new furniture, etc., or maybe there's a new cat in the neighborhood, your cat may be a little insecure and spray the wall or something nearby in order to say, "Hey, this is my territory."

So, figure out whether your cat needs a vet or a cat shrink. Your cat will thank you. 🐾

Do cat spray pheromones work to calm cats?

YOU'VE HEARD THAT CERTAIN pheromones help keep kitties calm, but do they really work?

In a word, yes. Cats will spray urine and scratch areas to mark their territory. However, in a study it was found that cats will not mark up places where cats rub with their facial pheromones, which is a natural calming scent to most cats.

Sprays and diffusers made with a synthetic version of these facial pheromones are extremely effective (95 percent). One study with sixty-one cats using the pheromones showed that by the twenty-eighth day, fifty-nine cats had stopped spraying urine altogether and the two holdouts no longer sprayed as frequently.

So you can either spray the pheromones, or rub your cat's face everywhere (but we guarantee the latter will cause stress). 🐾

Why do cats hate car rides?

OBVIOUSLY, BECAUSE THEY DON'T LIKE YOUR DRIVING.

But seriously, there are several reasons why most cats dislike car rides and get stressed out. The first may be that the cat may suffer from carsickness just like a person. (Hint: a vet can help you with that.) The second reason is that the cat associates riding in the car with traumatic events such as trips to the vet, trips to the boarding kennel, leaving his mom, etc. Let's face it, you wouldn't be thrilled with the car if all it did was take you to the doctor to be poked and prodded. Most cats are homebodies too, so anything that takes them away from home is stressful. Lastly, most cats just don't like the smell and sound of the car. It's noisy and gives off several unpleasant odors (just like Uncle Bob, huh?). 🐾

3

THE CAT'S HEALTH

Do male cats get sex-change operations?

FOR MANY CAT OWNERS, saving up for a sex-change operation for their cat just wasn't what they'd envisioned when they opened that Christmas fund account. But thousands of cat owners have done just that. It may not come as a surprise that the surgery is somewhat controversial.

Actually, though, these cats aren't trapped in the wrong-sex body; instead, they have a medical reason for needing their penis to be surgically removed. In feline urological syndrome (FUS), mineral deposits in the urine block the tiny passageway in the male's penis, causing urination to be difficult or impossible. When urine backs up the bad stuff in the urine also backs up, into the kidneys, causing kidney damage and a condition known as uremic poisoning. Left untreated, this can kill a cat quickly.

Cats with FUS may strain to urinate, often yowling as they try. They may try to urinate outside the litter box. Blood may be in the urine. As they get sicker, they just become quiet, sitting in a hunched up position. At this point it's a go-to-the-emergency-vet situation. The vet will insert a catheter so the urine can come out.

Special foods are available that have low ash and low magnesium levels, both of which have been implicated in FUS. Some foods also add acidifiers to keep the urine pH in the desirable normal range. Making sure the cat drinks a lot and eats moist rather than dry food also helps. But sometimes these measures are not enough.

Repeated episodes may cause scarring, which further narrows the passageway. For these cats, the answer is a sort of sex-change: a surgery called a perineal urethrostomy. The penis is shortened so that the remaining urinary canal is wider. This is a last resort because this also makes the cat more prone to urinary tract infections.

But don't worry; no matter what, he'll still be proud of his manhood.

If rabid dogs foam at the mouth, what do rabid cats do?

WHILE NO RABID CAT HAS STARRED in a horror movie, a rabid cat is a horror show, if only to himself. But do rabid cats foam and drool and attack, as rabid dogs are said to do?

Rabid animals often do drool excessively. But as we'll see later, usually not at the same time they're attacking. The drooling occurs because the virus causes painful spasms of the muscles that control breathing and swallowing, and swallowing eventually becomes so painful that the cat tries not to do so. Just looking at water can even cause painful spasms, which is how the word *hydrophobia* (fear of water) came into existence. The infected salivary glands also produce too much saliva, and since it hurts too much to swallow it, the saliva pools in the mouth and eventually drains out as drool or foam. This is complicated by the fact that as the muscles of the jaw become paralyzed, the lower jaw tends to hang open. Pretty, eh?

But just because a cat is foaming at the mouth, don't assume he has rabies (of course, if you don't know him, maybe you should assume it just to be on the safe side). Excessive foaming or drooling can be caused by a foreign object in the mouth, getting a bad tasting substance in the mouth (even getting too close to some toads will do it), or problems with the throat or tonsils.

Do all rabid cats attack? No. Rabies has three stages. In the first stage, which lasts two to four days, the cat may chew at the bite site, lose his appetite, run a fever, and exhibit some slight behavioral changes. It's in the second stage, which lasts two to three days, during which the cat may exhibit the mad dog, or mad cat, symptoms. He'll become restless, may roam, may lose fear of his natural enemies, and may attack anything, even inanimate objects. Finally, in the third stage, the muscles of the jaw and throat become paralyzed, his lower jaw tends to hang open, and he drools and foams at the mouth. The paralysis spreads to the rest of his body, and he dies. Some cats skip over the second stage and seem to go directly to the third stage, so not all rabid cats go mad. And attacking cats don't usually drool, since the two symptoms occur during different stages.

But if you see a cat foaming at the mouth and biting at anything that moves, don't try to second-guess things. Run away! Or, well, sneak away. And call the authorities. 🐾

Do cats get tonsillitis?

LIKE PEOPLE, CATS HAVE TONSILS, which are small masses of tissue in the throat that help protect the body from invading microbes. Because they're part of the body's immune system, they can swell when the cat is ill due to entirely other reasons. Repeated vomiting, coughing, or excessive swallowing from other causes can all bring on tonsillitis. But sometimes, tonsillitis is the primary problem.

Signs of tonsillitis are retching, coughing, head shaking, repeated swallowing, and fever. The tonsils are red and inflamed. Antibiotics are the first course of treatment, but sometimes cats must have a tonsillectomy. Break out the ice cream. 🐾

Can cats get AIDS?

YES AND NO. CATS CAN GET their own kind of acquired immune deficiency syndrome (AIDS), but you can't catch it from your cat by sharing needles with them, getting blood transfusions from them, or whatever other ways humans transmit AIDS from one person to another.

Feline immunodeficiency virus (FIV or FAIDS) is spread between cats by close contact such as biting, mutual grooming, and rarely, from mother to kitten. Sexual transmission does not seem to be an important means of transmission, if it occurs at all. In the

United States, about 1.5 to 3 percent of healthy cats are infected but have no symptoms. Like the human form (HIV), the virus that causes FIV is what's called a lentivirus, and it stays in the cat's body for many years before clinical disease manifests. So cats can be FIV-positive for years without having feline AIDS.

When AIDS does occur, the immune system becomes suppressed, and the cat is susceptible to infections of all sorts. The drugs used for humans with HIV or AIDS aren't used for cats because they cost too much, and because they often produce toxic side effects. But supplements to boost the cat's immune system may be helpful, and it's important to take preventive measures, e.g., keep the cat's teeth clean and keep him away from strange cats and other possible sources of infection.

The best way to avoid feline AIDS is to keep your cat indoors, away from strange cats that may harbor the virus. A vaccine is available, but it doesn't seem to protect against all strains of FIV to which cats may be exposed. One downside is that once vaccinated, feline AIDS tests will turn up positive for that cat, making it impossible until he starts showing signs to tell whether a vaccinated cat has actually caught the disease.

While AIDS is a very sad thing for your cat to have, don't be afraid of catching it from him (and don't be afraid of a cat catching AIDS from an infected person). It's a totally different virus from the one people get. 🐾

Can cats get leukemia?

CATS CAN GET LEUKEMIA, but it is very different from the leukemia that strikes humans. It is caused by feline leukemia virus (FeLV), which infects about 2 to 3 percent of cats in the United States, where it is responsible for more feline deaths than any other infectious disease.

The virus is found more often in outdoor cats than indoor cats, male cats than female cats, and younger cats than older ones. Because of its contagious nature, it's more common in multicat households than in single-cat households, especially when at least one cat goes outdoors.

FeLV usually spreads through infected saliva, but it can also be transmitted through urine, feces, blood, tears, and milk. It is passed through mutual grooming, bites, shared food/water bowls, nose-to-nose contact, shared litter pans, sneezing, and blood transfusions.

Cats may not show symptoms for months to years, but eventually, depending on the subtype of virus, may become anemic, immuno-deficient, or grow tumors. Most affected cats die within three years, but some live longer.

A vaccine is available, but it's not 100 percent effective. Although feline leukemia is incurable, infected cats can be helped with drugs such as interferon, ImmunoRegulin (an immune stimulant), and several others. 🐾

Can cats get heartworm disease?

FOR MANY YEARS, everyone thought that cats didn't get heartworms. Heartworms only happened to dogs. But that's not true.

Now we know that cats can also fall prey to these long, thin worms that take up residence in the cat's blood vessels and heart. Heartworms are transmitted by mosquitoes, and if your cat is bitten by just the right mosquito, even if he's an indoor cat and rarely even sees a mosquito, he can get heartworms. In fact, up to one-third of cats diagnosed with heartworms were reported to be exclusively indoor cats.

Heartworms are found in most parts of the United States, but are more common in warm, moist climates where mosquitoes thrive.

Compared with dogs, cats do have a natural resistance. They're only about one-fifth as likely to become seriously infected with heart-worms as are dogs in the same region. Unfortunately, when cats get heartworms, they tend to be much more adversely affected than when a dog gets them.

You can place your cat on heartworm preventive, but don't be tempted to use the dog's! Cats need a totally different dosage and should be tested to make sure they don't have heartworms before being started on the preventive, which is given once a month. And it's never too late or too early: Cats as young as one year of age and as old as seventeen have been diagnosed with heartworms. Don't let these little bloodsuckers worm their way into your cat's heart! 🐾

Can vaccines give your cat cancer?

BACK IN 1991, VETERINARIANS began to notice some curious things about a type of cancer called fibrosarcoma in cats. These are deeply rooted tumors that seem to dig into certain areas of the body; they often recur and behave even more aggressively after being surgically removed. They occur most often in the area between the shoulders, on the lower back, and upper thighs—the same areas that were being used at the time for most vaccinations. Their incidence increased in a community when local laws made rabies vaccinations mandatory. On the other hand, they were extremely rare in communities where cats weren't vaccinated. After extensive studies, scientists agreed there was something about the rabies and feline leukemia vaccines that seemed to increase the risk of a cat developing a fibrosarcoma in the area of the vaccination. Nobody knows why, but it seems to be asso-ciated with the fact that these vaccines use killed, rather than live, viruses. Such vaccines rely heavily on other components, called adju-vants, to help them work.

Does that mean it's safer not to vaccinate? No! The incidence of vaccine-associated fibrosarcoma is rare: somewhere between 1 in 1,000 and 1 in 10,000 vaccines administered result in a fibrosarcoma, which can appear anytime from one month to ten years later. Newer vaccines, such as recombinant vaccines, are being made that avoid some of the traditional adjuvants. Where possible, vaccines are being developed that don't require needles but can instead be sprayed into the nose. Veterinarians are careful to administer only the vaccines a particular cat needs rather than to bombard them with every conceivable immunization. And vaccines are administered into the cat's body only in places which, were a fibrosarcoma to develop, could actually be amputated were the cat's life in mortal danger. 🐾

Do cats get acne?

OH, THE TRAUMA YOUR POOR CAT faces when he has an outbreak of feline acne! But it doesn't just happen to cats in their high school years, or to cats that eat too many potato chips. Feline acne is a real and common problem for cats of all ages and breeds. At least, it doesn't seem to be attached to any kitty social stigmas.

Feline acne most often appears as blackheads on the chin and around the lips. They can form small scabby or draining areas. Nobody knows what causes it, but it may be influenced by stress, a suppressed immune system, poor grooming habits, or hair follicles that have abnormal amounts of oil within them. You can try treating it with antiseborrheic shampoos to break down the oils or even some topical vitamin A, as is used to treat human acne. Clean the chin after the cat eats, and switch to stainless steel or glass food and water bowls just in case he's one of those cats that is allergic to plastic.

And be sure he knows he's handsome, even with a few blemishes. 🐾

Do cats get appendicitis?

NO, BECAUSE CATS don't have an appendix. 🐾

Do cats get the flu?

CAT FLU ISN'T THE SAME AS PEOPLE FLU, but cats can get something called cat flu. It's actually a generic term for a group of infectious diseases that affect the upper respiratory tract, and less commonly, the lower airways. Sneezing, fever, and lethargy are the major signs, often with eye or nose discharge. It's contagious to other cats. But don't worry—you can't catch flu from your cat, and he can't catch flu from you. So if either of you is sick with flu, don't hesitate to cuddle up together in bed while you recuperate. 🐾

Do cats get hemorrhoids?

YOU MAY SEE YOUR CAT LICKING HIS BUTT or running around like his butt's on fire, and you may even see a swollen, reddened area on his anus. But cats don't get hemorrhoids, so while there's something definitely wrong, you need to look elsewhere for the answer. A bout of diarrhea can cause such symptoms, but they should go away within a day after the diarrhea is gone. If not, it may be something more serious, like impacted or infected anal sacs. 🐾

Can cats get impacted anal sacs?

ANAL WHAT? Unless you're a dog owner, you may not have heard of these delightful little sacs filled with the stinkiest substance known to man, situated just inside the anus on either side. Their function is to express a tiny bit of the thick goo every time your cat defecates, just to make sure it smells sufficiently bad. In dogs, they tend to get clogged up, and you'll see the dog scooting his butt on the ground in an effort to relieve the pressure. If the goo can't get out, it really hurts, and the sacs can get infected and even explode. OK, well, burst through the skin, although there won't be an actual explosion. The family cat usually looks on in utmost amusement at this typically disgusting canine malady.

Well, kitty, don't laugh too hard. Cats can get impacted anal sacs, too. They usually respond by licking their butt, over and over, until you eventually notice your cat seems to have a butt-licking fetish. But it's not all in his head—it's all in his butt, and you need to take him to the veterinarian and have the sac manually expressed.

By the way, since I know you're wondering: Don't worry, people don't have anal sacs. When your butt hurts, it's probably hemorrhoids. At least hemorrhoids don't explode. 🐾

Are natural products safe for cats?

JUST BECAUSE SOMETHING IS natural doesn't mean it's safe. After all, rattlesnake bites are natural. So are poisonous mushrooms. But what if products are not, in fact, harmful to people? Or even to dogs?

Still, the answer to the question is, not necessarily. Take the case of tea tree oil, promoted to treat skin problems and control fleas and other external parasites. It works, too, on horses and sheep. It works to help heal and soothe skin problems in cats, as well, and is found in some other products aimed at cats. But it's not actually safe for cats. It's absorbed into the skin quickly, and what's not absorbed gets licked off by the cat and ingested. So, cats and kittens have gotten sick, even died, from tea tree oil. Sometimes the so-called harsh chemicals, the ones that have had to pass all sorts of drug safety trials, are the safest. 🐾

CAT
CARE

Does tomato juice work on skunk odor with cats?

AH, THE AGE-OLD QUESTION: Does tomato juice work on skunk odor? Well, despite what you might have seen on old sitcoms, the answer is most positively, "No!"

You see, skunk odor is a mixture of oils and some stinky compounds called thiols. It's squirted from glands on either side of the skunk's anus (you wanted to know that, didn't you?). Skunks squirt when alarmed. So, when a cat is skunked, what do you do?

Well, let's look at the reason why tomato juice doesn't work. The thiols—which are associated with the same stench that comes from decayed bodies, rotten food, and poop—make up the smell. Tomato juice has nothing in its composition to counteract the smell. But what happens, interestingly enough, is that your nose gets overloaded because of the smell and, after a bit, you get used to it. It smells less bad because you've become desensitized. Sad but true.

Surprisingly, there's a homemade remedy that works really well. A chemist by the name of Paul Krebaum came up with this solution to chemically combat skunk odor. It consists of:

> 1 quart 3% hydrogen peroxide (fresh bottle)
> ¼ cup baking soda (sodium bicarbonate)
> 1 to 2 teaspoons liquid dish soap

You must mix it up at once and use it. Don't save any and don't store it in a closed container because it will explode. Don't get any in your cat's eyes, and rinse really well with water. Works like a charm. Maggie knows from firsthand experience. 🐾

Is homemade food good for my cat?

EVERYONE LOVES A HOME-COOKED MEAL—cats included. So, what's wrong with cooking for your cat every day?

Cats are obligate carnivores, meaning that they need to eat meat every day. Cat nutrition is different from people nutrition, or even dog nutrition. Cats need a certain amount of nutrients that are balanced. Too much or too little can be dangerous. In other words, just feeding your cat what you *think* is OK or on advice from anyone who doesn't have training in feline nutrition can be asking for trouble.

If you insist on feeding your cat people-food, you need to consult with a veterinary nutritionist who will help you balance the meals. After all, if you're going to all that trouble to cook for your cat, you ought to at least make sure the diet is properly balanced.

Can cats be vegetarians?

IF YOU'RE A VEGETARIAN, you're probably thinking of sharing your preferred lifestyle with your cat. After all, what harm will come from feeding vegetarian food to your kitty?

Think again. Cats are true carnivores and require the amino acid taurine in their diets. Taurine is found only in animal tissue, not plants. Without taurine, cats will go blind and have severe heart and reproductive problems as well as stunted growth of kittens.

But that isn't the end of it. Cats need arachidonic acid, and vitamins A, B12, niacin, and thiamin from meat sources because plants provide either very little or none of these nutrients or the cat's body can't metabolize the plant version properly. Lastly, cats need an extraordinary amount of protein (as compared to dogs) and can't ingest enough plant matter to get the amount of protein they require.

So if you insist on feeding an animal a vegetarian diet, we highly recommend you skip the cat and go with a pet that's made to eat plants, like a rabbit. Or maybe even a cabbit, if you can find one.... 🐾

Do cats need baths since they already clean themselves?

CATS SPEND A HUGE AMOUNT of time grooming, so do you really need to give a cat a bath? Well, maybe. Cats, like other animals, can become dirty, have flea infestations, or just smell bad. (If your cat has an odor, and you're not sure why, a trip to the vet might be in order.) So you don't necessarily need to bathe your cat unless she is dirty or unkempt in some way or is going to the cat show and needs to look sparkly clean. Or, as the comedian Steve Martin remarked, you just like hair on your tongue. 🐾

Can you use people shampoo on a cat if you need to?

PEOPLE SHAMPOO, CAT SHAMPOO. But if you read books that cat writers write, you'd think you'd be hurting your cat by using people shampoo on her.

Well, sometimes. Let's say you're out of a pH-balanced cat shampoo, and all you have in the house is the shampoo you've been washing your hair with. Your cat comes home dirty. Do you wait or use the shampoo?

Go ahead and use the shampoo, but don't use it all the time. A special pH-balanced shampoo for cats won't dry out his skin and coat the way a human shampoo can. 🐾

Should you let your cat roam?

AT ONE TIME, PEOPLE used to let their cats run loose all the time. The idea was that a cat needs to go outside. Even now, there are people who allow their cats to wander all over. Is this a good idea?

Of course not. Loose cats can come in contact with other stray cats and pick up incurable diseases like feline leukemia, feline AIDS, and even rabies. Cats can kill wildlife, destroy property, get into garbage cans, and create a nuisance. On the human side, a cat that is loose can get hit by traffic, eat dangerous or toxic things like rat poisons and antifreeze, get lost or stolen, get shot at, or even fall victim to cruel and evil people bent on doing it harm.

Believe it or not, there are fences designed to keep your cat in. So if you'd like to let your kitty explore the great outdoors, but in a controlled way, consider a cat fence. It'll make for a safer environment. 🐾

Are table scraps OK for a cat?

YOU'RE SITTING DOWN TO DINNER, and before you know it, your cat is right there begging for a taste. What should you do?

Say yes, but within moderation. Table scraps, often the inedible portions of meat and vegetables, can be pretty tasty to cats. Problem is, table scraps are low in vitamins and usually loaded with calories, high in fat, sugar, and salt—things your cat really doesn't need. So feeding your cat a large amount of table scraps is a bad idea.

However, many veterinary nutritionists recommend that if you have to give your cat treats, you should try cooked vegetables (no onions) or cuts of lean meat and make sure that the percentage is no more than 5 percent of your cat's total caloric intake for the day. That way, your cat can enjoy tidbits and still remain healthy. 🐾

Do indoor cats miss being outside?

ALTHOUGH WE CAN'T ASK A CAT whether she wants to be outside or not, our best guess is that cats, especially those that have been indoor-outdoor cats, do indeed long for the great outdoors. But the great outdoors is fraught with perils, including cats with diseases, cars, dogs, predators, and people intent on doing a cat harm.

There are two ways to deal with your cat's yearning for the great outdoors. One is to provide enough activities indoors to make it fun and interesting enough for her. The second is to provide careful containment for the cat that wants to go outdoors. There are many different outdoor cat enclosures and fences that remove some of the worry about your kitty sating her wanderlust. The outside cat enclosures are like huge cages with climbing things in them or are like enclosed tents with mesh that your cat can travel through or sit in. The cat fences are much unlike a regular fence (most cats find regular fences laughable) in that they look unsteady and therefore dangerous for a cat to climb on.

In most cases, what an indoor cat doesn't know won't hurt her. And an indoor-outdoor cat may find the great indoors far more interesting than the outside. So keeping your cat indoors or in a controlled enclosure is the right thing to do. 🐾

Can you change a cat's name?

YOU'VE JUST ADOPTED A CAT. The problem is, someone already gave him the name "Fluffy"—which you're none too keen about. Can you change your cat's name without any serious repercussions?

How would you know? We suspect the cat really doesn't care. After all, most cats don't come when their names are called anyway, so changing your cat's name from Fluffy to Stardust, Mitzy, or Queen of All She Surveys, probably doesn't matter much. Maggie's own cat, Hailey, knows and answers to her name, but she also answers to other names, too, so we really can't say it makes a huge difference. 🐾

Is catnip like marijuana?

YOU'VE SEEN CATS WITH CATNIP. They act crazy after a few whiffs and rub in it and drool. But is it addictive and harmful to the cat? And does a cat really get high from it?

Catnip is one of those plants with a lot of folklore surrounding it. Many cats love catnip and either go crazy over it or may actually fall asleep with it. However, not all cats are affected by catnip. Kittens younger than six months, for example, don't react to catnip, and some adult cats don't have the genes that enable them to enjoy catnip.

Catnip contains nepetalactone, which makes cats react the way they do. The reaction is pretty short-lived, however, and cats usually stop reacting after a couple of minutes. Your cat will enjoy a fresh bit of catnip, but don't inundate her—she can build up a tolerance to it. If your kitty used to love catnip and doesn't anymore, try hiding the toys with catnip for a few weeks and reintroduce them to her again later.

Contrary to folklore, catnip isn't addictive, nor is it harmful. Because cats can build up a resistance to it, more doesn't do anything. Catnip, when made into a tea, is soothing and relaxing to people but has none of the same effects demonstrated in cats.

So your cat won't need a twelve-step program, after all. 🐾

Can an older cat bond with someone?

WHEN PEOPLE THINK ABOUT GETTING A CAT, they think primarily about getting a kitten. After all, a kitten is cute and will bond with the new owner. But what about older cats? Do they bond with their owners too?

The answer is a resounding, "Yes!" Cats do bond with people, and adult cats will bond with people as well as kittens do if given enough attention and love. 🐾

5

Cat Senses

Can cats follow a scent trail?

TRUE, YOU MAY NOT SEE A pack of cats on the trail of an escaped convict, but that doesn't mean they couldn't do it. They're cats. They just don't *want* to do it. But give them a reason (a mouse trying to sneak past, for instance) and they can follow a scent trail just fine.

Despite their tiny noses, they have a strong sense of smell. The inside of their nasal cavity is made up of an intricate network of bony surfaces covered with olfactory epithelia. The more olfactory epithelium, the more area for olfactory receptor cells. You have about 4 square centimeters worth of olfactory epithelium, and your cat has about 40 square centimeters. That's more than some dogs—the Pekingese has only 20 square centimeters. As far as the number of receptors, cats have about 60 million, compared with your paltry 6 million. But before you offer up your cat's services to the local police force, don't get too uppity. German Shepherds have about 170 square centimeters of olfactory epithelium and 220 million receptors.

Of course, cats use their noses in a way that is more familiar to people: avoiding bad food. Unlike dogs, who seem to relish rotting garbage, cats seem particularly sensitive to smells containing nitrogen compounds—the odor of rancid foods. Maybe that's why your cat sticks his nose up at the food you let sit there all night, while your dog scarfs it up even after you thought you threw it in the trash!
Kittens appear to imprint upon a particular teat, seeking it out by its smell, so that by the time it is two to three days old, each kitten has suckled exclusively from its own personal nipple. That decreases sibling rivalry over who gets to sit where at the table! 🐾

Are there any cat repellents that work?

URINE SPRAYING BY CATS, especially male cats, is one of the greatest complaints of cat owners. However, a curious thing was noticed about where cats sprayed: They never sprayed places that had been previously marked with facial pheromones. (These are the scents that cats leave behind when they rub their face on surfaces.) Scientists were able to make a synthetic version of these odors, and they found that when applied to a surface, cats wouldn't spray there. It also made the cats stop scratching those surfaces, and generally seemed to calm them down in stressful situations. The product, called Feliway, would seem to be a miracle invention.

Does scratching on furniture and wood really sharpen a cat's nails?

SOMETIMES. When they scratch on your good furniture, they're doing it in order to leave their scent and mark that as part of their territory—sort of like saying, "Muffy was here." They'll revisit the area regularly, not to completely destroy your belongings but because one good scratch deserves another, so to speak. That is, the scent from their previous escapade makes them feel the need to do it again.

While scratching is more behavioral and territorial, it does help to sharpen the nails, although that isn't the primary reason why cats scratch.

Is it true that if a cat's whiskers can fit through a hole, the rest of her body can?

IN THE NATURAL STATE, YES. The cat has about twenty-four vibrissae (the real name for cat whiskers) on each upper lip, plus a few other feelers on each cheek, over the eyes, on the chin, and even on the back of the wrists. They're much thicker than regular hairs and are embedded three times more deeply with extensive nerve endings. They can pick up swirling air currents, vibrating as air eddies around objects, allowing the cat to feel things almost without touching them.

The upper two rows of vibrissae on the upper lip can move independently of the bottom two rows. Nerves from vibrissae lead to a specially marked area of the brain that has some similarities to the visual center, leading some researchers to speculate that cats can practically "see" with their whiskers. In fact, the vibrissae appear to play an important role in hunting, since a cat with damaged vibrissae may bite the wrong part of a mouse it's attacking. That's because when prey is close to the cat's mouth, its vibrissae actually move forward to feel the prey, probably helping the cat to know the location of its parts, even when the mouse is too close to the cat's mouth to see.

When navigating narrow passageways in the dark, the vibrissae spread out so that the cat can judge whether it can fit through an opening. Unfortunately, the vibrissae don't grow longer when the cat grows wider, so fat cats can be misled!

Incidentally, when you feed a cat from a bowl so narrow that its vibrissae touch the sides when she eats, she may refuse to eat. That may be why so many cats remove their food from their bowls and eat it on the floor. 🐾

Do hairless cats have whiskers?

HAIRLESS CATS, such as the Sphynx breed (which are, more accurately, "almost" hairless, as they are covered with what can be called a light "fuzz"), may have full-length, short, or no whiskers at all. 🐾

Why do some cats make a funny face when they smell certain things?

YOUR CAT IS SNIFFING AROUND the bushes when, all of a sudden, he opens his mouth and makes a funny face. What the heck is he doing now? This response occurs most often when a cat is smelling the urine of another cat, so think about it: Wouldn't you make a face if you'd just stuck your nose where somebody had peed? Only the cat seems to enjoy the experience, and there's more to it than making a face. He's actually making use of a special sensory organ you don't have, called the vomeronasal organ. When he holds his mouth slightly open, and perhaps opens and closes it slightly, he's performing what's called the Flehman response, in which he samples an odor (often female urine) and forces a bit of it into a tiny passageway in the roof of his mouth just behind his front teeth. That passageway connects his mouth and nose, and in between is the vomeronasal organ, which seems to be specialized for detecting whether a female cat is in heat. So when your cat, especially your tom, is doing this, just think of it as looking at a centerfold. Oh, wait—I meant reading the articles.

Why don't cats like sweets?

BECAUSE THEY CAN'T TASTE THEM! In fact, scientists have shown that the entire cat family lacks one of the two proteins inside their taste receptor cells needed to detect sweetness. They traced this back and found it was caused by a mutation that must have occurred very early in the evolutionary history of the cat family. It may have been adaptive because cats are obligate carnivores and so need to eat a mostly meat diet to maintain good health. Since meat isn't sweet, as are some plants, it would be better for the cat's nutrition if they weren't enticed by plant foods that were sweet. I wonder if I can get that gene spliced into me.

Do cats like artificial sweeteners?

CATS NOT ONLY DON'T CRAVE SUGAR, they don't appreciate the millions of dollars of research invested in creating artificial sweeteners. Scientists can record a taste bud's response to various flavors, and in doing so with cats found out that, unlike human taste receptors, cat taste receptors don't respond at all to artificial sweeteners. I have to agree with the cats on this. 🐾

Does a cat's eye color affect its vision?

ALL KITTENS ARE BORN WITH BLUE EYES, but as they mature, other pigments rise to the iris surface so that most adults have either green, yellow, orange, or blue eyes. Blue-eyed cats are usually either white or pointed (Siamese patterned). Cats can even have one blue eye and one eye of another color. But so far, nobody has been able to find any difference in vision related to eye color. That's the case with people, too, so maybe it shouldn't be a surprise. What is a surprise is that eye color can be associated with deafness, at least in white cats. 🐾

Why do cats have slit pupils?

ONE MINUTE YOUR CAT IS looking at you with those oh-so-cool cat eyes with the vertical slit pupil, and the next she's almost got wide puppy dog eyes with big round pupils. What gives? Cats, foxes, and a few other species that are active in a wide range of light levels often have slit pupils. The beauty of a slit pupil (besides looking neat) is that no other pupil shape affords the great range in size. In bright light, it constricts to a tiny slit, much smaller than any round pupil can manage. And in dim light, it opens to a huge round shape. So the reason cats have slit pupils isn't because they're active at night (nocturnal) animals, but because they are both diurnal (active in daytime) and nocturnal animals. And because they look cool. 🐾

What is a third eyelid?

HAVE YOU EVER PRIED OPEN your cat's eye while she was sleeping? No? Well, that's good. But if you did, you'd see a thin translucent cover that closes from the inner corner of the eye. It acts as an extra protector, and is technically called the nictitating membrane. You may also see it if your cat is ill or just sleepy. Or if she grows a third eye. 🐾

Can cats see in color, or do they see just in black and white?

YOUR CAT SEES COLOR, but not like you do. Your eye makes use of three types of color receptors, each maximally sensitive to a different wavelength of light, either short (red), medium (green), or long (blue). It's the same concept your television uses; if you stick your face up close to it you can see tiny dots of red, green, and blue lights. But seen together, these three hues make up all the colors you see. Your cat not only has fewer of these receptors overall than you do but is missing the green one (although some research indicates it may have a very few green receptors). That's similar to the situation with certain red–green color-blind people, mostly men, who are called "deuteronopes"—they're missing their green-sensitive cones. They see greenish-blue colors as white or gray. They can tell the difference between blues and reds, but often confuse hues ranging between greenish-yellow and red. Even if the cat does have some green-sensitive cones, their sense of green and its influence on discriminating color mixtures is probably minimal. In addition, because the cat has so few cones overall, the intensity of the color, as well as how detailed it is, is very low compared with ours. The moral of the story? Never let your cat pick out your socks. He is not handing you those unmatched pairs as a fashion statement. 🐾

Do cats need glasses?

IF YOUR CAT LOOKS AT YOU from across the yard like you're some kind of a space alien out to abduct her, she may have good reason—she may not be able to make out who you are, at least not by sight. Cats don't have 20/20 vision. In fact, their vision is somewhere between 20/100 and 20/200. That means they can just barely make out details from 20 feet away that a person with good vision can make out at 100 to 200 feet away.

Before you rush out and try to fit your cat with glasses, there are two things you need to know. First, it's not so much a problem of being nearsighted or farsighted as much as it is the fact that cat eyes are adapted to see in dim light, not to make out details. It's the result of a big pupil, lots of rod receptors instead of cones, and a reflective, light-scattering layer behind the retina. So glasses won't help. The second thing you need to know is that cats refuse to answer when you try to get them to read the charts. They're stubborn like that. 🐾

Can cats really see in the dark?

NOBODY CAN SEE IN ABSOLUTE DARKNESS, but a cat makes it seem that way. Cats have a minimum light detection threshold up to seven times lower than that of humans. Cats' eyes have several features that help them see well with just the tiniest amount of light. First, they have large, round corneas—that's the clear part at the front of the eye. They're larger than yours, and collect more light that way. Second, they have larger, rounder lenses within their eyes than yours—also to collect more light. Third, their pupils can widen more than yours, letting in more light. Fourth, they have more rod receptors compared with cone receptors than you do. Not only are rods more sensitive to dim lights, but many rods pool their responses, so that lots of very dim lights add up to one pretty dim light. Fifth, they have a reflective layer, called the tapetum, behind the receptors that acts like a mirror, redirecting any light that has passed by the receptors back into them for a second chance at reception. The cat's tapetum reflects up to 130 times more light than does the back of the human eye.

They do a pay price for their ability to prowl around effortlessly as you trip and curse over furniture. Everything I just mentioned that makes the cat's eye better at seeing under dim lighting, makes it worse at detecting fine details. And remember, all those rods exist at the expense of the cones, making cats' color vision pretty weak—a separate question we answered on page 69. 🐾

Can cats "hear" through their eyes?

I READ THIS ON A CAT FACT LIST: "In the dark, cats' eyes function more like ears, because their pupils pick up acoustic vibrations." Let's see, how do I answer this scientifically? Oh, I know: Balderdash! 🐾

If a cat has its lens removed because of cataracts, does it need a lens implant?

YOU PROBABLY DON'T HAVE TO worry about this, because unlike dogs and people, cataracts aren't so common in cats. But occasionally they do get them, and the lens must be removed so that the cat can see clearly. But if you just remove the lens and don't replace it with a fake one or with glasses like they do in people, how clearly can the cat really see? It turns out, not very well. Without a lens, a cat would need to wear glasses that had a strength of more than 15 D—far stronger than you'd find on the drugstore rack. Since cats are too vain to wear glasses anyway, the surgeon must implant an intraocular lens when the real lens is removed. 🐾

Can cats watch TV?

MOST CATS APPRECIATE A television set more for its warmth than for its entertainment value. But a television image presents certain impediments to a cat's viewing pleasure. The images on a typical television are refreshed sixty times per second—so often that they appear to be a continuous picture to us. But a cat can detect the flicker of a light that is refreshing as quickly as seventy times per second, suggesting that the television image would appear jumpy to her.

Nonetheless, the right program—usually something with contrasting moving shapes—often does get the attention of some cats, especially young ones. Most older cats probably learn that the images on the screen aren't real, and furthermore come to realize that today's television programming leaves much to be desired for someone of discriminating taste. 🐾

Do cats' eyes glow when they get angry?

WHEN A CAT IS EXCITED IN ANY WAY, his pupils automatically dilate (get big). The same thing happens when he's in the dark. And the same thing happens with people. If you shine a light directly into that big pupil, you can get a glimpse of the back of the eye. In a person, the back of the eye is covered with blood vessels, so it just looks red. That's what accounts for red-eye in flash photography. But in a cat, the back of the eye has an extra layer of shiny cells called the tapetum. The tapetum isn't there just to look sparkly, or to scare us at night. Its function is to reflect any light that may have slipped past the retinal cells back into the retinal cells for a second chance to be detected. It's one of the reasons cats have such better night vision than we have. The dog also has a tapetum, but the cat's is made up of more highly reflective cells, and many more layers of them, so it's much shinier than the dog's. The tapetum lies behind the retina and in front of the blood vessels, so when you shine a light directly into a cat's eye, you see this bright, shining reflection. If you take a flash photo of your cat, you'll see it may be shiny yellow, green, or orange. The color isn't like a mood ring's color; a cat keeps the same color reflection whether he's happy, bored, or angry. Some cats with pale blue eyes are missing their tapetum; if you take their picture, instead of eye shine you'll see red—just like the red-eye you get when you take a flash photo of a person.

By the way, glowing eyes don't necessarily mean he's mad or in attack mode. They just mean he's excited—OK, maybe because he's mad, or in attack mode. 🐾

Do cats with strangely shaped ears have poorer hearing than other cats?

MOST CATS HAVE PRICKED EARS, which act like your cupped hand to amplify and direct sounds down into your ear canal. They can swivel their ears independently so that they point to the front, side, or back, and they can pinpoint the source of a sound so accurately that they can judge within 3 inches the location of something a yard away.

A few cat breeds have unusually shaped ears. The Scottish Fold has ears that are bent over forward, forming a cap over the ear canal; American Curls have ears that are curled slightly backward. Although no studies comparing their hearing have been performed, it stands to reason that their outer ears are not funneling sounds optimally. But they can still put your hearing to shame! 🐾

Do silent dog whistles work for cats?

CATS CAN HEAR SO-CALLED silent dog whistles, which are really only silent for humans and some other acoustically challenged species. Ideally, dog whistles emit a frequency between 23,000 and 54,000 Hz, although some emit frequencies as low as 16,000 Hz (which people can hear). Since a cat can hear frequencies up to 64,000 Hz, which is approximately 1.6 octaves above the human range and one octave above dogs', they can readily hear dog whistles. But they probably won't pay any attention to them. That just wouldn't be cool. 🐾

Can cats hear those ultrasonic pest deterrents?

ULTRASONIC PEST DETERRENTS are supposed to drive pests, not pets, out of your home. Fortunately, they don't appear to work for either. These devices emit sounds typically at frequencies between about 32,000 to 65,000 Hz. So while they're well above the human hearing range, many, if not most, of them are well within the cat's range, which consists of frequencies up to 45,000 Hz. And you wonder why he acts crazy? 🐾

Do cats suffer from thunderstorm phobias?

DOGS ARE NOTORIOUS WHEN it comes to being phobic in regard to loud noises, like gunshots and thunderstorms. But what about cats? It turns out that while cats can be frightened by loud noises, they only rarely become unhinged as some dogs do. Maybe that's because their natural response is to hide, whereas a dog's is to, well, just act stupid. Actually, one researcher believes dogs are more susceptible to static electricity during storms because of their large size, and thus tend to panic when storms develop. Cats just wait out the storm, then strut out, look at the frantic dog, and make fun of him. 🐾

How does a cat know how high to jump?

IT MIGHT SEEM LIKE THEY use some sort of kitty sonar, but as far as we can tell, cats judge distance just like the rest of us do—only somehow, they seem better at it. Like ours, a cat's eyes are placed facing forward. Compare this with most dog eyes, which are placed somewhat obliquely on the head, or with horse or rabbit eyes. Animals that need good depth perception tend to have eyes that face directly forward. It has to do with how the two eyes see slightly different angles of the same object; the closer that object is, the more the two views of it differ. Try it yourself by holding your finger in front of your face at different distances and then watching the image jump back and forth as you close one eye and then the other. The closer it is, the more it jumps, because of the greater or lesser difference in the viewing angle. So when your cat jumps on top of your dresser from the floor, he's subconsciously judged the distance by comparing the input from each of his eyes. Cover one eye up, and watch him crash and burn. (Well, he'd actually still do a fair job using other cues, and even if he did make a mistake, he'd pretend he planned it that way.) 🐾

Why do cats with certain coat patterns tend to be cross-eyed?

MOST CROSS-EYED CATS are those with either Siamese-pointed patterning or an albino-white absence of coloring. These cats have abnormal pathways from their retinas to the visual areas in their brain.

Here's the difference. Say a normal cat is looking at a mouse some distance in front of him. The visual receptors in his right eye and those in his left eye see that mouse from a slightly different angle. The nerves from each of those receptors are routed through the optic pathways so that some stay on the same side of the brain as the eye they came from, and some travel to the opposite side, all so that the nerves leading from the two receptors with their two slightly different angles of the mouse can converge on the same spot in the brain.

That spot can compare those teensy differences in the angle and derive an estimate of how far away the mouse is.

What's this got to do with Siamese and albino-white cats? The nerves from some receptors don't cross over to the opposite side of the brain as they should, and essentially what happens is that the brain gets input from a receptor in the eye that sees the mouse, but not from the other eye, which is seeing the window. So the brain has to ignore some of the input, and it ends up not being able to use the binocular cues it should. Now, not every nerve is misrouted; more are misrouted in albinos than in pointed cats. And these cats seem to manage fine as they are. But when tested carefully, they have less visual acuity and less binocular vision than normal-colored cats. Without that binocular feedback, the eyes can become crossed, or perhaps they become crossed simply in an attempt to match up some visual fields from those few areas that do align.

So the next time you see a Siamese or albino cat acting weird, you're perfectly correct to just shrug your shoulders and say, "His brain's not right." 🐾

Do cross-eyed cats see double?

PROBABLY NOT. Most cross-eyed cats also have abnormal visual pathways, such as those of Siamese-patterned or albino-white cats (see the previous question). When images from the two eyes don't agree with one another in the brain, the input from one is overpowered, or suppressed, by that of the other. Eventually, the brain may even develop a new line of communication with each eye, letting the cat have stereoscopic input even though the eyes are not aimed at the same spot. This happens only if the cat has been cross-eyed since kittenhood. In fact, most cross-eyed cats can use input from both eyes to achieve good depth perception, and you'd never know from the way they can jump nimbly from one perch to another that their vision is in any way abnormal. 🐾

Are white cats deaf?

FIRST, JUST BECAUSE YOUR CAT is white and doesn't listen to you doesn't mean he's deaf. But, he might be. Whiteness in cats can be caused by different genes; it's only the dominant white (W) gene that is associated with deafness. A cat with one W gene is white; a cat with two W genes is also white, but has an additional chance of having blue eyes or of being deaf in one or both ears. There also appear to be two different types of blue eyes. The vivid blue associated with Siamese and Oriental cats doesn't seem to be associated with deafness. It's only a W white cat with light blue eyes that seems predisposed to be deaf.

Studies of white cats in breeding colonies have shown that about 12 percent of all W white cats are deaf in one ear, and 39 percent are deaf in both ears. Of the cats whose parents are both white, the percentage of affected cats goes even higher—sometimes as high as 96 percent. The percentage of deaf white cats is much higher in those with blue eyes; 85 percent of cats with two blue eyes are deaf in one or both ears, 40 percent of cats with one blue eye are, and 17 percent of white cats with non-blue eyes are. These estimates are higher than you would find just randomly checking white cats off the street, however, because the parent cats in these studies were preselected for their likelihood of being deaf. 🐾

Is it hard to live with a deaf cat?

WHAT'S THE DIFFERENCE? They don't listen to you anyway! But OK, they do come running when they hear the can opener, or the knife on the cutting board, and a deaf cat can't do that. But cats have such well developed senses otherwise, many people living with a deaf cat never even realize their cat is deaf. Those who do figure it out teach the cat to come by tapping (or stomping) on the floor, and they're careful not to let the cat outside where she could fall easy prey to dogs or cars. And don't feel sorry for such auditory-challenged felines—very likely most of them are glad they don't have to listen to our baby talk. How degrading! 🐾

Why are kittens born with their eyes closed?

DURING THE FETAL DEVELOPMENT of all mammals, the eyelids grow together and temporarily fuse closed over the eyes. Animals, such as those with hooves, that need to get on their feet and get going soon after birth, are born at a more mature stage; their lids have already opened by the time they're born. Humans, too, have lids that are fused while in the womb but that will have opened by the time of birth. Kittens and many other mammals, however, still have their lids fused together at birth. The kitten's lids won't open for another ten to fourteen days. The rest of the kitten's eye isn't developed yet either; the retina is still immature, although it can respond to light.

Some kittens can get eye infections beneath the closed lids. The areas start bulging with discharge that can't escape. A veterinarian can treat this condition by, among other things, partially opening the lids so that medication can get to the eye. Opening the lids early does not seem to hurt the cat's later vision. But don't try this at home! 🐾

Can newborn kittens see, hear, smell, or taste?

A NEWBORN KITTEN HAS an immature nervous system, but it matures rapidly over the next few weeks. During a kitten's first two weeks of life, her world is dominated by things she can feel, taste, and smell.

A kitten can feel whether she's too warm or too cold, and will try to crawl toward or away from a source of heat to adjust her temperature. She can't otherwise regulate her own body temperature until about three weeks of age and won't be able to do so as well as an adult until about seven weeks old.

She's born with eyes and ear canals closed, but she's not blind or deaf. Although the ear canals remain closed until about fifteen days of age, she can respond to sounds by five days of age. By four weeks of age, she will orient to sounds just like adults do.

And she can react to bright lights even though her lids are still closed. Even after her eyes open, her vision still won't be clear. By the end of the third week of age, however, she can find her mother by sight. Fully functional vision won't be present until she's about a month old. Even then, her acuity isn't great; it will improve sixteen-fold between two and ten weeks of age, and will continue to improve gradually, up to three to four months of age.

6

Q
CAT
EMOTIONS
A

Do cats mourn?

IF YOU'VE EVER HAD A loved one die, you know how it feels: It's an empty feeling in the pit of your stomach that you can't ignore. You feel sad and depressed. In other words, you mourn for the loss of that person.

But can cats feel a sense of loss and mourn? Do they get depressed when an owner or another cat passes away?

Most definitely. Cats make friends and become used to people and other animals just as we do. So, when that person or animal dies or goes away, a cat will stop eating and act depressed. The cat may look for that person or other animal in the places she expects them.

So yes, it seems cats do indeed feel grief and can mourn. 🐾

Can you trust someone your cat hates?

YOU'VE HEARD THE OLD ADAGE of never trusting someone your pet dislikes. But if your cat dislikes your new boyfriend or Aunt Edna, should you say goodbye to them?

Maybe, or maybe not. It really depends on what your cat doesn't like about them.

Cats are great observers. Cats have developed amazing powers of observation that would rival Sherlock Holmes. They observe things that you and I might never notice—a person's posture, certain reactive smells (such as those that accompany fear, anger, or being relaxed), facial expressions, and other things cats look for when sizing up a person or a situation. Your cat already knows the emotional state of the person who visits even before he or she says a word. Your cat will be quick to pick up on whether the person is anxious or fearful—or even if he doesn't like cats. Your cat reacts according to what he sees and smells. If he doesn't like it, he doesn't like the person.

This works pretty well if you have a bad guy who is intent on doing harm. His body posture, combined with his scent, can be a signal that he is up to no good. However, this scent thing can get a bit out of hand. Let's say your Aunt Edna smokes cigarettes or your boyfriend decides to try some new aftershave to impress you. Your cat may decide he doesn't like the cigarette smell or doesn't like the aftershave, and may be associating that scent with something threatening.

While cats can be astute judges of character, they can, like other creatures, occasionally be misled. So, just because your cat hates them, it doesn't mean these are bad people. It may just mean that your boyfriend needs to change his aftershave, not overhaul his personality.

Do cats have friends and enemies?

WE ALL KNOW WHAT IT'S like to have friends. We also know what it's like to have enemies—or at least, people we don't like. But can cats have friends and enemies? The answer is—yes.

While domestic cats are mostly solitary, many feral cats live in cat colonies where they can interact with each other. Some cats consider other cats buddies and friends, just as we would.

So, what about enemies? Oh yes, cats can certainly hate other cats. All you have to do is hear a cat squabble in the middle of the night to figure that one out!

Do cats feel jealousy and spite?

"HE DID THIS TO SPITE ME!" How many times have you heard a pet owner say that, when their cat has scratched their sofa or sprayed on a wall? Or maybe there's a new boyfriend or a new baby in the house. You may be thinking that cats feel jealousy and spite, in spite of themselves.

Spite (which causes people to do something tit-for-tat) is a pretty complex emotion: It requires us to see some behavior we don't like and to conceive of doing something totally different that will irk the other person. For example, a teenage girl might not like the way her brother teased her the other day, so she hides her brother's backpack to retaliate. That's spite. However, cats don't think that way.

A cat associates a particular occurrence with what is going on *right now*. Your cat scratches the furniture while you're gone. You may think he's "getting back at you" for being gone so long. Actually, what is happening is that your cat needs to scratch, and the couch is a convenient scratching post. He may be feeling a bit stressed out over your being gone. He scratches it because it feels good. You come home, discover your couch scratched up, and get angry. Your cat is left puzzled and dismayed that you came home and punished him. See the problem?

What about jealousy? Cats can feel as though they aren't getting enough attention, certainly, but they don't associate their rambunctiousness with anger or spite. Instead, they react to the lack of attention by trying to draw your attention toward them, using good or bad means.

So, instead of thinking your cat is doing something to spite you, try to see that your cat may need more attention and more training. 🐾

Do cats fall in love?

WE'VE ALL SEEN THE DISNEY movies where a boy cat meets a girl cat and they fall in love, such as in *The Aristocats*, but do cats fall head-over-paws in love with other cats? And is it really romantic?

We know that cats do indeed make friends, and many are boyfriend/girlfriend type relationships. But is it love?

Cats don't mate for life. In fact, if a female cat comes into season (heat), you can guarantee that all the male cats, regardless of their love for their current feline "girlfriend," will be homing in on the new female. After all, it's instinct and hormones. So, the concept of falling in love goes out the window right there.

However, that doesn't mean that cats can't feel some affection for one another that goes beyond the physical. Maggie has seen several cases where cats that lived with each other seemed to bond more closely than with others. Was it love, or just a passing fancy?

Well, sadly we can't ask a cat if he or she has ever had a heart-throb, so the question is completely debatable. Maggie thinks that cats can have strong feelings towards other cats, but whether it is "love" leaves much up to the interpreter. So, the answer is: maybe.

Do cats cry?

YOU'RE SITTING DOWN ON A Saturday afternoon watching those sappy old movies and bawling your eyes out. Your cat may be watching it alongside you, but never sheds a tear. Or maybe he does. Do cats cry?

Cats' emotions aren't tied to their tear ducts. While cats do get teary-eyed, they do so because there is some sort of irritant in their eyes. Other conditions that can irritate the eye include tumors, eye infections, and upper respiratory diseases.

So, if your cat is shedding a tear or two over a movie, it's time for a trip to the veterinarian for an eye exam.

Do cats get embarrassed?

IT'S HARD TO IMAGINE AN ANIMAL who licks his private parts as one who might get embarrassed. But oddly enough, cats appear to become embarrassed when something happens that they didn't intend.

Maggie has seen cats do silly things and then act like there was nothing wrong. Her own cat, Hailey, woke everyone up from sleep at 3:00 AM when she tried to jump on the counter and knocked a dish to the ceramic floor, causing it to shatter into a million pieces. When Maggie's husband went downstairs, Hailey was sitting with her back to the mess and staring hard at a (rather boring) box, as if this was the most interesting thing in the world. You could almost imagine her whistling innocently.

Is there actual proof of cats being embarrassed? Well, embarrassingly enough, they haven't the ability to tell us, so we really don't know. But there's a good chance that they do.

7

CAT
BREEDS

Are there really cat breeds?

YES, THERE ARE CAT BREEDS. Both the Cat Fanciers' Association and The International Cat Association (TICA) recognize at least thirty-nine breeds. These cats are called *pedigreed cats* (not purebreds) because they have a definable pedigree that includes an admixture of cats from other breeds. The only true purebreds are Turkish Vans, Siamese, Japanese Bobtails, and Abyssinians, which technically have no other breeds mixed in. 🐾

Why do Manx cats hop?

MANX CATS ARE OF A tailless or near-tailless breed with larger and stronger hind legs than other cats. When running, these cats can sometimes exhibit a hop, because of their powerful hind legs. 🐾

Are Siamese more vocal than other cats?

YES, GENERALLY. Siamese cats tend to be talkers, as are most Oriental breeds. 🐾

Do Siamese cats all have kinks in their tails?

NO, ALTHOUGH SIAMESE CATS from Thailand may still have a kink in their tails. Many Siamese cats bred in the United States have been bred not to have kinks in their tails. 🐾

Are all Siamese cats cross-eyed?

NO, AND HERE'S WHY: Crossed eyes are considered a fault in Siamese, and have been bred out by conscientious breeders, though some cats still exhibit crossed eyes. The reason why Siamese cats had crossed eyes was to compensate for other eye defects produced by the albino allele, which produces colored points. 🐾

Are Ocicats part ocelot?

LOOKING AT AN OCICAT, you may be thinking that the Ocicats have ocelot or painted leopard in them. However, you'd be wrong.

Ocicats originated in 1964 when a breeder crossed a Siamese with an Abyssinian in an attempt to create a Siamese with Abyssinian points. The first generation all looked like Abyssinians, but some of the second generation had spots. Later crosses with American Shorthairs were made to enhance the contrast of spots in some colors.

Breeder Virginia Daly's daughter nicknamed the breed Ocicats after ocelots, and the name stuck. But, there are no wildcats in their background, other than typical cats that act in a wild fashion.

Is there really such a cat as a Munchkin?

YOU MAY HAVE SEEN little cats with stubby legs and were told that they were Munchkins. "Come on," you think. "Is there a cat breed of that name?"

There is a group of cats called the Munchkin Breed Group, which have a genetic variation (some would call it deformity) of the long bones in the legs. This is a form of dwarfism in cats. Several registries ban Munchkins because many consider it cruel to breed a cat with these variations, but they are recognized by TICA.

Most Munchkins behave like normal cats but have shorter legs. Still, there's a fair amount of controversy surrounding whether or not such cats should be intentionally bred for such dwarfism.

What's the biggest cat?

THE BIGGEST DOMESTIC CAT would probably be the Maine Coon. With some cats weighing twenty-five pounds or more, they can be bigger than some dogs.

What's the tiniest cat?

THE SMALLEST CAT BREED is the Singapura. Most females weigh about four to six pounds, and most males weigh six to eight pounds. 🐾

Are there really hairless cats?

YOU MAY HAVE WATCHED the Austin Powers movies and seen Dr. Evil's cat, Mr. Bigglesworth, who is a hairless cat. But are there really hairless cats?

Well, sort of. Mr. Bigglesworth is a cat from the Sphynx breed. The Sphynx cat is about as hairless as they come, but can be covered with downy hair. Some light hair is often present on the nose, tail, and toes. People often describe petting a Sphynx as petting a warm peach or a hot water bottle wrapped with chamois. 🐾

Is DSH/DLH a breed?

DOMESTIC SHORTHAIR (DSH) and domestic longhair (DLH) are both just another name for moggies, that is, standard, run-of-the-mill cats. They are no more a breed than mutts are for dogs. 🐾

What's the prettiest cat?

BEAUTY IS CERTAINLY in the eye of the beholder, so it's tough for us to truly say which cat is exactly the prettiest. But if you want show winners, take a look at the Cat Fanciers' Association winners. The judges chose GC, BW, NW Melositos White Owl of D'Eden Lover, a white Persian, as the best cat that most conformed to the standard for 2006 to 2007. 🐾

8

THE SEXUAL CAT

Do cats get stuck when having intercourse?

UNLIKE DOGS, CATS DON'T GET stuck when having sex. But that doesn't mean the act is entirely comfortable, at least if the female's reaction is any clue. And is it any wonder? The male cat's penis is covered with tiny barbs that point backwards, so when he withdraws it, it scratches against the sides of her vagina. Ouch! That's got to hurt.

By the way, a neutered cat's penis loses its barbs.

Why do cats make so much noise when they mate?

YOU WOULD, TOO, if a barbed penis were involved. But actually, it may not be the barbs that stimulate the female to yowl during intercourse. In a scientific study (and I swear, I am not making this up), researchers measured the length of erect cat penises and found the average to be about 5 mm. The scientists then inserted a 4 mm probe into a receptive female cat, and found that when it reached the cervix, the cat yowled. The scientists concluded that what makes the female yowl during sex is the penis distending the posterior vagina. Who says science isn't fun?

Can a litter have more than one father?

DURING THEIR RECEPTIVE PERIOD of estrus, female cats can be very, very receptive—sometimes mating with fifteen different males over a three-day period. The female won't ovulate until she's been bred by the first male. Stimulation by the male's barbed penis causes the release within minutes of a certain hormone, which in turn causes ovulation to begin around twenty-four hours later, lasting to about thirty-two hours postmating. Any other male that breeds with her around this time is as likely to father her kittens. A study of free-roaming city cats versus country cats showed that 70 to 83 percent of city cat litters had more than one father, compared with 0 to 22 percent of country cat litters. No, city cats aren't loose compared with country cats! They just have more mates to choose from, since many of the country cats have only one male around. 🐾

Are there paternity tests for cats?

PATERNITY TESTS DO EXIST for cats, but at present they have been used principally for research. However, as more genetic tests exist for hereditary cat diseases, cat breeders are having their cats "DNA fingerprinted" so they can prove paternity through cat-specific DNA tests. Unlike within the dog world, however, cat registration bodies do not allow litters to be registered to more than one sire. 🐾

Do cats have preferences when it comes to a mate?

DURING THEIR RECEPTIVE PERIOD, female cats can be, um, quite receptive. But they still have limits. In one study, females who were courted by between 9 and 19 males, bred only with 3 to 9 of them. Older females tended to be less choosy (sigh), as were those who were courted by fewer males (sigh again). Females were more likely to reject closely related males than unrelated or distantly related males. After all, they have to respect themselves in the morning.... 🐾

What's a teaser tom?

IMAGINE IF YOU WERE A MALE and your job was to service females, who were brought to you from all over, but who would never get pregnant. Such is the sad life of a teaser tom, the gigolo of the cat world. He's a vasectomized (not neutered, or castrated) male, sometimes a retired stud, who still has the urge to mate and still has the barbs on his penis that stimulate ovulation. Breeders bring their in-heat females to him to mate with in order to induce them to ovulate, and thus come out, and stay out, of heat for a reasonable period of time. Without being bred, the female will stay in heat for one to two weeks, and come back into heat two to three weeks later, over and over. Not only is this a nuisance, but it's bad for her reproductive system, increasing her chance of a uterine infection called pyometra. So the teaser tom is sort of like a doctor, practicing preventive health care. Yeah, sure. 🐾

Can cats be artificially inseminated?

WHEREAS MOST RESEARCH dealing with cat reproduction centers around how to make it stop, some research has also made advances in helping cats reproduce. Actually, artificial insemination was first described for cats more than thirty years ago, but it's still not commonplace. However, because it's just not easy to keep a stud cat around the house, more breeders are freezing the sperm of genetically valuable cats and then neutering them. Semen can then be inseminated in the female through the vagina or by way of surgery.

The greater challenge is collecting the semen from the tom, and he's not always that cooperative. While you can generally take a dog to the veterinarian and induce him to have at it into an artificial vagina, not even mood music, magazines, or videos are enough to get the average tom in the mood when away from home. Actually, in dogs, so-called digital manipulation is often enough to get him in the mood; I would not advise trying this with a cat. Some male cats have been trained to use a tiny artificial vagina, which is slipped into place while he's in the act of mounting a female in estrus. This is not easy. Instead, most semen collections are done with the male cat anesthetized, using a method called electroejaculation. It must be performed by an experienced reproductive veterinarian. A small rectal probe is placed up the cat's rectum and delivers a mild electric current.

This stimulates the nerves, causing ejaculation. Now, please note I said *anesthetized* male. I do not advise sticking things up the rectum of any wide-awake cat! Also, please note I said *mild* current. We are not talking cattle prod here. Finally, please guys, as fun as this sounds, don't try this at home. 🐾

What is stud tail, and do you want it?

ALTHOUGH THIS SOUNDS LIKE the sort of disease men wouldn't necessarily mind admitting to having, it turns out it's not related to having lots and lots of sex, not even if you're a cat.

Stud tail occurs when the sebaceous glands at the base of the tail are overactive and so become plugged with blackheads. It's like feline acne of the tail. And although it's most common in intact males (possibly because the glandular activity of the supracaudal organ near the base of the tail may be testosterone-dependent), it's also seen in females and neutered males.

No, you don't want it. 🐾

Are some cats homosexual?

HE MAY LOOK LIKE A TOUGH TOM, but do you really know who he's hanging out with in that alley? Chances are, cats can be bisexual. Researchers have found examples in more than 450 species, including cats, of some sort of same-sex courting, or other behavior commonly thought of as homosexual. Male cats often mount one another in what appears to be an imitation of sexual behavior. Such behavior may not be sexually motivated, however, but rather a sign of dominance or play.

Still, that doesn't mean that cats of the same sex cannot be sexually interested in one another. In intact males especially, the urge to have sex is strong and could involve other household cats. 🐾

Do cats masturbate?

YOU COME HOME, fling open the door, and catch your cat in an embarrassing predicament. He's got his arms around a stuffed toy, kneading it with his forefeet and straddling it with his hind end. Or he's on his back, rolled forward, his little paws playing with his new toy between his legs. He's masturbating, but don't worry—he won't go blind. God won't smite any kittens, and it's entirely normal behavior for intact male cats. Just knock before you come home next time. 🐾

Do cats miss sex once they're fixed?

HOW WOULD YOU KNOW? They don't go out and rent more kitty porn. But if we can extrapolate from other species, female cats almost certainly don't miss sex when they're spayed, for the simple reason that they are interested in sex only when they're in estrus, and spaying prevents estrus from occurring. Neutered males that are sexually experienced, however, may continue to show mating behavior for several years following castration. Most male household cats are neutered before experiencing the joys of sex, and these cats probably don't miss sex because they don't know what they're missing. However, if they're given testosterone replacement therapy after castration, and placed with a female in estrus, they may or may not mate with her. I'm not really sure why anyone would give a cat testosterone replacement therapy, however. Perhaps the cat was too well behaved? 🐾

Do neutered cats spray?

BET YOU ALREADY KNOW THE answer to this question. About 25 percent of single-cat households experience urine spraying, as do about 100 percent of households with ten or more cats. Urine spraying makes up almost half of all house-soiling complaints. Most of those cats, especially the ones in single-cat households, are probably spayed or neutered. Sure, spraying is the signature of the tomcat, but neutered males—and even females, intact or spayed—don't mind practicing a little forgery now and then.

Toms usually mark their territory by spraying urine on vertical surfaces. The behavior begins around the time they reach sexual maturity. Females tend to spray mostly when they're in heat. Neutering reduces spraying behavior in both males and females, but may not be as effective if the cat has already made it a part of his daily repertoire. If done before sexual maturity, it reduces or eliminates spraying in 90 percent of neutered males. Cats tend to spray more when they are stressed, crowded, or feel themselves in competition with other cats, so alleviating these conditions may help lower your stress, as well.

Does neutering a cat make him get fat?

NOTHING IN LIFE IS FREE, and all the good that comes from neutering comes at a price. You may get a fat cat. When researchers studied metabolic rate, using heat production as a gauge, they found that castrated males needed an average of 28 percent fewer calories than intact males. So if you have a castrated male, you may need to cut back on the cat chow.

Do cats go into menopause?

INTACT FEMALE CATS REMAIN fertile throughout their lives, although they tend to have smaller and fewer litters, and less chance of raising them successfully. The oldest known cat to have kittens was a thirty-year-old feline named, imaginatively, "Kitty." Several cats in their twenties have successfully reared litters, usually consisting of only one or two kittens. So just because she's old doesn't mean she can't attract a beau—or that she doesn't have to worry about an "unplanned pregnancy." 🐾

How many kittens can a cat have?

"TOO MANY" IS THE OBVIOUS ANSWER: Cats were created to go forth and multiply, and they are extremely good at it. Mothers have eight teats, and they typically have about five or so kittens. One exceptional cat named Tarawood Antigone gave birth to nineteen kittens, of which fourteen were born alive and survived. She didn't even take fertility drugs.

Cats can begin reproducing by six to eight months of age, and left to their own devices, tend to have litters in the spring and fall. If their kittens die before being weaned, the mother will usually come back into estrus sooner, and so could have more kittens to make up for her loss. The most kittens reported were from a single mother named Dusty, who was born in 1935 and had her last litter when she was seventeen years old. She gave birth to a total of 420 kittens. 🐾

Should cats get blood tests before becoming parents?

THERE MAY BE A BETTER REASON for cats to get blood tested before mating than for people to do so before marriage: The wrong match of blood types can mean unhealthy or even dead kittens. It's called blood group incompatibility. Cats have, for practical purposes, two blood types: A and B (a third type, AB, is very rare). Kittens receive one blood-type gene from each parent, with the gene for Type A dominant to that for Type B.

Here's where it gets tricky. All Type B cats carry an anti-A antibody, and about one-third of Type A cats carry an anti-B antibody. An anti-A antibody attacks Type A blood cells, and an anti-B antibody attacks Type B blood cells. When a cat has kittens, antibodies in the mother's milk can cross through the kitten's gut during its first sixteen hours of life. If the milk carries one of these antibodies to the kitten's blood type, the antibodies will attack the kitten's red blood cells. This causes anemia, jaundice, and death; or in less severe cases, the kitten's tail-tip falls off.

Because 95 percent of mixed-breed cats in the United States are Type A, most mothers and kittens share the same blood type and no problems occur. In purebred cats, blood type depends on the breed. Some breeds, such as Siamese and their relatives, have no known Type B individuals. Others, such as the Rex breeds and the British shorthair, have from 30 to 59 percent Type B individuals. If a Type B female is bred to a Type A male, some or all of her kittens must be removed and bottle-fed for these first sixteen hours. The same holds if a Type A female carries a recessive Type B gene and is bred to a Type B male or a Type A male with a recessive B gene. If there's a chance of incompatibility, you can blood-type the kittens using blood from the umbilical cord, and compare the type of each kitten with the mother.

But modern science has once again stepped in to simplify things. A new DNA test is now available, so instead of testing a blood sample, you can simply rub a swab on the inside of your cat's cheek and mail it in for analysis. And I'm just sure your cat will sit still for that little exercise—right? 🐾

Is there such a thing as identical twins in cats?

MOST CATS ARE BORN AS PART of a litter, so in that sense, they're essentially fraternal twins, triplets, etc. A few, however, are probably identical twins—probably, because the only real way to tell is through a DNA test. Looking alike or having identical markings isn't good enough. Identical twins come from the same fertilized egg that splits and becomes two separate embryos. Depending on when the split occurs, the twins may share a placenta (the later the split, the greater the chance they will share one placenta), but not always. Some breeders have reported kittens being born with only one placenta between them, but there's always a chance that two kittens are born one after another and that one placenta has become detached and only been delivered later. It's also possible that two placentas can grow together and appear as a single entity.

Strangely, the strongest evidence for identical twins in cats comes from the occasional appearance of conjoined twins. Conjoined twins are usually identical twins that have failed to separate entirely, or they may be fraternal twins that fused during a later stage of development. Because most reported cases of conjoined kittens seem to involve animals of the same sex and physical characteristics, chances are they are conjoined identical (Siamese) twins.

By the way, identical twins would not necessarily share the same markings, since certain identifying characteristics, such as the size and placement of spots, are determined during in-utero development by random cell splits. 🐾

Can kittens be conjoined, like Siamese twins?

I SWEAR I'M GOING TO SKIP ALL the obvious Siamese cat quips. Conjoined kittens have been reported at least since the 1700s, and no doubt existed well before then, but were seldom reported, for superstitious reasons. Severe cases, such as six-legged or even eight-legged or two-headed cats, essentially two-bodied cats, rarely survive past birth. Some less severe cases do survive, such as "Stumpy" and his twin, "Stumpy." They were attached at one leg, so the farmer simply chopped it off, creating two stumpy-legged but healthy cats. I guess there weren't that many good names to go around. 🐾

Do some cat breeds need Caesarean sections?

SOME BREEDS OF DOGS ARE notorious for needing Caesarean sections for delivering their puppies. Although far less common in cats, some cat breeds are more likely to need C-sections than others. Both brachycephalic (flat-faced) and dolichocephalic (long-faced) cat breeds are more likely to need C-sections than cats of more conventional head types. Specifically, the Devon Rex has been reported with the highest incidence of C-section deliveries, at 18 percent. 🐾

Are all calico or tortoiseshell male cats sterile?

THE SHORT ANSWER IS: no. The medium answer is, most are, but a few aren't. The long answer is, well, as follows.

In the cat, the gene that decides whether the coat color is orange or black is located on the X chromosome. A male cat has one X and one Y chromosome. The X can carry the gene either for black or for orange, but not both. A female cat has two X chromosomes, so it's possible that one can carry a gene for black and the other for orange. In females, the X chromosome does something other chromosomes don't do: Because animals don't do well with extra copies of chromosomes, and since all you need is one X chromosome (as in males), one of the X chromosomes in each cell is randomly inactivated at some point during development. A female cat with one X chromosome carrying the orange gene, and one carrying the black gene, would have, at random, one of the X chromosomes turned off, so the cat would have a random mosaic of orange and black cells for its fur. Thus, the cat ends up with random patches of black and orange, or tortoiseshell. White is carried on a different chromosome, and its inheritance is unrelated. All you need know as far as it's concerned is that if the cat has white overlaid over its tortoiseshell coat, it's a calico.

But if a cat has to have two X chromosomes for this to work, and a male cat has only one X chromosome, how does a male tortoise-shell come to be? These males, instead of being XY like normal males, are very often XXY. This condition is not uncommon in animals. Humans with XXY are said to have Klinefelter syndrome; they are typically sterile. However, rare cases of fertile tortoiseshell males have been reported.

These rare fertile tortoiseshells appear to have the normal number of X chromosomes, so they are, like normal males, XY. However, their splotched coat arises from another phenomenon, called a somatic mutation. During development, a mutation can occur in the cells giving rise to fur color, which in turn produce cells of that same color. Such cats are called mosaics. It's much like a birthmark, or a mole, on your skin. So a cat may have one or more patches of black fur, which arise from a mutation, in addition to the orange fur his genes coded for. When bred, he will produce offspring as though he were a regular orange cat. 🐾

Can cats have Down syndrome?

NOT REALLY. Cats normally have 38 chromosomes, but just as with people, some cats occasionally end up with an extra one or two. We're most familiar with trisomy-21, an extra copy of human chromosome 21 which results in Down syndrome. People, as well as cats, can have extra copies of other chromosomes, too. In humans, an extra X chromosome causes Klinefelter syndrome, which also occurs in wild and domestic cats. The most apparent sign of an extra X in a cat is a male tortoiseshell. Some Klinefelter cats (which are always males) may be unusually large—as well as unusually loving. This, however, is not the same as Down syndrome, which can technically only occur in humans. 🐾

Have genetically engineered cats really been developed?

ACHOO! Wouldn't you give just about anything not to be allergic to your beloved pet? A lot of people have said just that, and back in 2004 there was a plan to genetically engineer a hypoallergenic cat. The plan was to do away with the gene that causes the production of a protein called Fel d1, which is responsible for most of the cases in which people are allergic to cats (about 10 to 20 percent are due to allergies to two other cat proteins, albumin and cystatin). Fel d1 is secreted by sebaceous glands and is found in cat fur, saliva, urine, and mucus. The plan initially was to use genetic engineering to insert a less common gene variant that does not produce Fel d1. However, in the end, the folks at Allerca went back to doing it the old fashioned way: selective breeding. However, they used a new-fashioned twist: They used DNA to identify the cats with the divergent gene that produced a nonallergenic version of such cats. Now, one can be yours for the low, low price of $3,950! But wait, that's not all! If you act now, they'll throw in spaying and neutering. Actually, you'll get that whether you want it or not. Did you really think they were going let you start breeding them after all they invested? 🐾

Can cats be cloned?

THE FIRST CLONED COMPANION ANIMAL was born on December 22, 2001. The kitten, named CC (for Carbon Copy) was a white cat with gray tabby markings, and her mother was a calico cat named Rainbow. But wait—shouldn't CC have been a, um, carbon copy of Rainbow? Both cats shared identical DNA, but because some characteristics, such as the distribution of color patches, depend on chance events during development, a clone will never be absolutely identical. In fact, CC is said to be more outgoing and more svelte than her comparatively retiring and rotund DNA donor.

That didn't stop bereaved cat owners from lining up to be among the first to try cloning their beloved cats—although the $50,000 price tag managed to stop most. Still, Genetic Savings & Clone, the only company cloning cats commercially, produced five cloned kittens for owners who thought once was not enough. The company was able to offer clones on sale for only $32,000. Even this bargain-basement price tag failed to attract sufficient customers for the company to turn a profit, and in 2007 Genetic Savings & Clone died a natural death. 🐾

Can domestic cats interbreed with wildcats?

JUST BECAUSE YOUR CAT THINKS he's a tiger doesn't mean you should let him get any ideas about friskying up to the next bobcat lass he sees and trying to make babies. He's more likely to be served up for lunch. But does that mean it's genetically impossible to cross a cat with a bobcat? Or, for that matter, what about a tiger, leopard, or any other species of wildcat?

In fact, domestic cats have been interbred with a variety of small wildcat species. The best known result of such a cross is the Bengal cat, which derives from a domestic cat crossed with an Asian leopard cat. The Safari cat is the product of breeding a Geoffrey's cat with a domestic cat. Hybrids have also resulted from human-arranged crosses with the margay, little spotted cat, jungle cat, and caracal, among others. Several fairly convincing reports exist of hybrids from the northern lynx and bobcat, but these have not been confirmed.

Don't think you can just pair off your domestic cat with one of the small wildcats, though. Even the small wildcats tend to kill domestic cats unless they themselves were raised with them. Then there are size as well as chromosomal and gestational differences to contend with. Some of the so-called small wildcat species are actually pretty big. Servals run to about 30 to 40 pounds. Not only can they purposefully kill a prospective mate, but the mechanics of getting things lined up can be dicey. Assuming all goes well, there is then the matter of chromosome number. Domestic cats have 38 chromosomes. Hybrids can occur between species that have almost the same number of chromosomes, but the offspring are often infertile. Of the 23 species of small cats studied so far, 18 of them, including the leopard cat, also have 38. But some, including the margay, ocelot, and Geoffrey's cat, have 36. The first-generation offspring of a domestic cat and a Geoffrey's cat have 37 chromosomes, for example, and are not always fertile. Then comes the matter of gestational period. A domestic cat carries her kittens for 63 days. The bobcat, leopard cat, and lynx all have gestation periods within a few days of that. But some wildcats carry their young longer. A serval, for example, carries her kittens for 74 days. If the dam is the domestic cat, she will have given birth to kittens that tend to be premature (for a serval) and may not survive. If the dam is the serval, the kittens develop for 74 days, but when born are more the size of domestic kittens, and may not be accepted by the dam. When you get to the big cats, gestation times get much longer; for example, the tiger carries her young for 103 days. So even though the tiger and cat share the same number of chromosomes, their pairing is just not going to work. The take-home lesson? When it comes to crossing domestic cats with wildcats—don't try this at home. 🐾

Is there really such a creature as a cabbit?

I RECENTLY RECEIVED A CALL from a friend asking where she could get a cabbit, a creature that is half cat and half rabbit. She'd heard of a company in America that is selling them, but they have a long waiting list for these beautiful, affectionate animals. When I seemed a little doubtful, she carefully explained (slowly, because I was obviously not up on scientific advances) what the company had said: that cabbits are possible because male rabbits will mate with just about anything, the two species have approximately the same gestation period, females cats will raise just about anything, and cats and rabbits share the same number of chromosomes.

This theory has several problems. First, male rabbits can't mate effectively with female cats (OK, they can mate, but the rabbit's penis lacks the barbs necessary to stimulate the female cat to ovulate; however, I suppose it would be possible for the cat to mate earlier with a male cat, thus stimulating her subsequent ovulation). Second, cats have far fewer chromosomes than rabbits (38 chromosomes in the cat, 44 in the rabbit; however, some other species can still interbreed with even greater differences in chromosome number). Third, the rabbit's gestation period is much shorter than the cat's (31 days for the rabbit, 63 days for the cat). Last, but certainly not least, cats and rabbits are not only of different species, but belong to different orders (Carnivora and Lagomorpha, respectively). This last one is the biggy. Hybridization occurs only between closely related species. Hybridization between different species is rare enough, but it's never been known to occur between species of different orders. That would be the same as a person and a pig having babies. Don't you think such an event would be all over the news?

So-called cabbits are more likely cats with the tailless or bobtail gene combined with another genetic deformity that causes the loose skin along the flank to be tucked up tight to the belly. This causes the already long hind legs and rounded rump seen in many Manx-type cats to look even longer. The fact that some Manx cats hop when running only makes the idea seem more plausible.

Who started this fanciful feline fallacy? Another of those newfangled Internet rumors, no doubt. In this case, we can actually trace the originator, one Joseph Train of Castle Douglas, Galloway. He wrote about it in his book *An Historical and Statistical Account of the Isle of Man,* published in 1845. I guess he was just ahead of his time.

So where can you get a cabbit? Try a magician's hat. 🐾

Do squittens exist?

LIKE CABBITS, other fanciful critters called squittens are supposed to be the offspring of cats and squirrels. But do they exist?

Well, assuming a cat could mate with a rodent, why would it want to? (Rather eat the rodent, right?) And even if you have a truly lovesick tabby, those schooled in basic biology know that the genetic makeup of both is completely incompatible. So just as *you* can't have kittens, neither can a cat have squittens—it just doesn't happen.

But what if your cat has kittens with a gray coat and a bushy tail, and no other prospective suitors match the description besides that pesky squirrel? Look to your basic alley cat—gray is a common recessive dilute color in cats, and when recessive genes get put together, you can get gray.

The other so-called squitten trait is exhibited by cats with radial hypoplasia. This is the same genetic defect one sees in so-called twisty cats and kangaroo cats. It's a type of dwarfism that shortens the cat's forelegs.

So, no, your cat didn't have squittens. No matter what your friends tell you. 🐾

9

FELINE INTELLIGENCE

Do cats think?

NO ONE WHO HAS LIVED WITH a conniving cat has ever, for one moment, paused to consider the possibility that they don't think: Of course they do—just look at how they outwit you on a daily basis! Cats even manage to look thoughtful, even if all they're thinking about is, well, nothing.

But how do we really know if that look is one of thoughtfulness or just thoughtlessness? The problem is, it's hard to know if *anyone* thinks, much less somebody who communicates only in a language we barely understand. For centuries, philosophers maintained that only humans could think. Anything a cat did that seemed smart, they said, was no more the product of thought than the fact that a plant grows toward the sun.

In the early 1900s, a scientist by the name of E. L. Thorndike placed cats in what he called a puzzle box, where the cat had to press a lever or pull a string to get out of the box and get a reward. At first, the cat would learn by sheer accident, so-called trial and error, but once he got it right he would quickly learn the magic trick that allowed him egress. Because the cat didn't seem to use any insight, some people used this as evidence that cats don't think. They later compared this with experiments in which monkeys had to use tools and pile up boxes to reach a hanging treat. The monkeys didn't use trial and error but instead would study the situation for a long time and then seem to say "Eureka!" and instantly do what it took to get the treat.

The problem was that there was no way anyone, even a monkey, could study Thorndike's puzzle box and come up with a solution; even a person would have to use trial and error. So for decades following, cats continued to be unjustly thought of as thoughtless.

Scientists are still looking for a good way to prove that cats think. But whatever they come up with, it won't be as convincing as simply living with a cat. 🐾

Can cats recognize themselves in a mirror?

WHEN KITTENS FIRST SEE THEMSELVES in a mirror, they typically react as though they're meeting another kitten. They may sniff, arch their back, and try to walk around and investigate the back of the mirror. With time, however, they seem to grow tired of this scentless new kitten that silently mocks them. Is it that they realize it's some sort of trick, or do they understand it's a reflection of themselves? That would be important news for scientists interested in animal thought, since the ability to recognize oneself in a mirror is frequently cited as evidence of higher order consciousness.

Behavioral scientists study this question in human babies and animals by placing a mark on the subject's head, one he can't feel, and then watching for his reaction when he spots it in a mirror. By two years of age, human children will act surprised, then reach for the mark. Dolphins, killer whales, great apes, and elephants also investigate the mark, by turning to view it at different angles or by touching it. Cats, alas, do not. Or maybe they're just too cool to let you catch them gazing at themselves admiringly in the mirror. Just imagine what they do in front of it when you're gone. 🐾

Can cats be mentally deficient?

CONTRARY TO THEIR OWN BELIEFS, cats aren't actually the smartest beings in your home. OK, some are. But most cats do an assortment of amazingly stupid things, even if they won't admit it.

But just as with your other family members, some may be a little slower than others. And while we can't test our cat family members on standardized IQ tests to see if they're really suffering from some kind of learning disability, there are some cats that just don't seem to catch on to normal cat things the way you expect a cat to do.

The truth is, like people, cats have normal variation in intelligence. Genetics plays a role, as do early mental stimulation and experiences. Certain chromosomal disorders can lead to slow behavior in cats, just as trisomy-21 (Down syndrome, which is caused by an extra chromosome) does in people. However, few people are going to have their cat's chromosomes tested, so the extent of this type of mutation isn't known.

Brain injury can also cause mental slowness. Kittens with hydrocephalus have abnormal pressure on their brain, and while they can survive into adulthood, they almost always have learning deficits for the rest of their lives.

Fortunately, cats don't have to graduate from college, or even trade school, in order to have a bright future. All they need is you, loving them for what they are. 🐾

Can you train a cat?

ANY LION TAMER WILL TELL YOU, of course you can train cats! And of course, they still may not always do what you tell them.

You can train your house cat just as readily—and a lot more safely. After all, cat actors routinely perform all sorts of stunts and behaviors to star in movies and cat food commercials. And your cat has taught himself how to pull your strings to get what he wants. True, the typical cat isn't begging for the chance to heel, sit, and stay. Cats aren't dogs, and some of the forceful training methods that used to be so popular with dog trainers simply didn't work with cats. But if you use positive, reward-based training methods (which are also more effective with dogs), cats can be eager and gifted students.

Cats have been trained to do just about any trick a dog can do and can also run an obstacle course. Many owners teach their cat to use the people toilet, even flushing it afterwards. Now if they could just teach those boy cats to put the seat back down when they're through... 🐾

Can cats count?

IF YOU TAKE A KITTEN AWAY from a litter when the mother cat's not there, she'll notice. How? Does she count them? If so, what if she had a really big litter? How high can a cat count?

Chances are, mother cats notice a kitten is missing not because the count is off, but because they recognize each kitten as an individual and notice the absence of a particular kitten. Or it is indeed possible that mom has a general conception of "how many," and when one is missing she does in fact realize something is wrong. Scientists have shown that dogs realize when an expected quantity is off, such as when one treat plus one treat equals three treats, but no such experiments are available for cats.

A cat named Cutey Boy was said to be mathematically gifted, supposedly adding, subtracting, and even solving algebra problems. He would bump his nose against his owner's face a number of times to indicate each number. For larger numbers, he would twitch his tail and look at a card that had the correct answer on it.

If Cutey Boy had just counted to three, it would be impressive, and even convincing. But the fact that he could work out square roots in his head made it more likely something else is going on. Remember Clever Hans, the remarkable counting horse? It turned out that his handler was subconsciously cuing him to give the right answer. Oh, by the way, Cutey Boy also was said to understand eight languages. 🐾

Are some breeds of cat really smarter than others?

IF YOU WANT TO START A CAT FIGHT, put cat owners in a room and ask them which breed is the smartest. There's no way they'll ever agree. Some rankings list members of the Oriental breeds, like the Siamese, as the smartest, but that's probably because they're the most active, thus giving the impression of being more curious and intelligent. Remember, a truly smart cat will never let you know just how smart he or she is. 🐾

Are cats smarter than dogs?

LET'S SEE, DOGS PULL DRAFT CARTS, stay out for weeks at a time guarding sheep, and get shot in the line of duty. Cats, um, well, sleep in the sun and meow while you fix their dinner. That pretty much answers that question, as far as I'm concerned.

But actually, it probably merely reflects the evolutionary fact that dogs are social animals and cats are solitary animals. It's adaptive for dogs to follow orders, so to speak, whereas the cat's ancestors were never in that situation. A cat naturally answers to no one, other than herself.

Cats don't tend to do as well in maze tests as dogs do, but that, too, is just part of being a cat. A cat naturally explores small places, like blind maze arms, and when a cat is stressed, it often stops and grooms, which tends to make her time in the maze seem very long. In fact, some cats just take a snooze in the maze! After all, somebody will come take them out eventually!

So cats don't do what you say. That in itself seems pretty smart to me. 🐾

Do cats understand it when you point?

HOW OFTEN HAVE YOU pointed to something you wanted your cat to see only to have her stare at your finger? Or more likely, just ignore you. Cats, like many animals, don't grasp the concept of pointing. And why should they? There's nothing in their evolutionary history that would make it adaptive to follow where somebody was pointing. After all, when was the last time you saw a cat point and say, "They went thataway"? Or maybe they just know it's not polite to point. 🐾

Can some foods make cats smarter?

THERE JUST MAY BE A reason that smart cats eat fish. It's brain food. Certain types of fish contain high levels of omega-3 fatty acids. Human children born to mothers who had taken cod liver oil during pregnancy and lactation scored higher on a mental processing test at four years of age compared with children whose mothers had taken corn oil. Omega-3 fatty acids have even been implicated in reducing criminal behavior. One recent study found that supplementing the diets of poor children in Mauritania with higher quality food, including fish, which contain omega-3 fatty acids, reduced their criminal activity when they got older. Another recent study found that adding fatty acid supplements to the diets of adult prisoners decreased prison violence.

Less controversial are studies that looked at maze learning in puppies. Puppies fed various levels of omega-3 fatty acids were subsequently trained to associate a symbol, either a cube or a sphere, with the correct direction to take in a T-shaped maze. Those fed the higher levels performed better. While no amount of nutritional supplements is going to get your cat to run a maze or even come when called if he's not in the mood, at least he might think about it. 🐾

Do cats understand the concept of time?

YOU KNOW YOUR CAT HAS A concept of time; he knows when you usually get up in the morning, so he times his pillow tromping and hair pulling for about a half hour earlier. He knows when you're one minute late serving his supper, so he threatens to hit the speed-dial number to report cruelty to animals.

It's hard to know how our sense of time compares with our cats', but we do know that you can give them the best watch in the world and they'll scarcely bother to glance at it. The problem is, scientific studies of feline time perception are rare. What we do know is that cats are adept at learning what's call *fixed interval responses*; that is, if you give a cat a task to do, such as pressing a lever, but reward him for it only precisely every half hour (or any other period of time), the cat will quickly figure out the time interval, laze around in between time, and when the time approaches, start frenetically pressing the lever. In fact, in one study, cats learned they would get rewarded for pressing a lever only at one particular time of day. So they slept and played, and as the time approached, they stretched, leisurely walked over to the lever, pressed it halfheartedly a few times, and then settled in to get to work, pressing it like they were sending Morse code until they got their meal. Then they took a bath and went back to lounging for the next twenty-four hours. How long is that in cat hours? 🐾

Do cats get Alzheimer's?

DOES YOUR CAT WALK AROUND IN A DAZE? Has he suddenly forgotten where the litter box is? Or what it's for? Maybe he gets lost outside or forgets to groom himself. Can cats become senile? Actually, yes. Very old cats can suffer from a type of senility known as feline cognitive dysfunction syndrome (FCDS).

In fact, behavior problems in general aren't uncommon in older cats. More than half of cats over the age of eleven have at least one behavior problem that started in old age, and by the time you get to cats older than fifteen, about 80 percent have developed some behavior problem. But behavior problems aren't the same as senility. If you look just at cats that tend to be disoriented, the condition is extremely rare in cats under the age of fifteen. However, 40 percent of cats over the age of sixteen have periods of disorientation.

Dogs with cognitive dysfunction can be given drugs for treatment, although the drugs aren't always effective. No such drugs are currently approved for cats, but some cats appear to benefit from the same drugs that dogs take. If the drugs don't work, well just humor him. He's earned it.

10

MISCELLANEOUS QUESTIONS

Do cats really see ghosts?

SINCE NEITHER CAROLINE NOR MAGGIE believe in ghosts, this question was especially hard for us to answer. However, Maggie has a friend, the world-famous cat author and ghost expert Dusty Rainbolt, author of *Ghost Cats: Human Encounters with Feline Spirits* and *Cat Wrangling Made Easy* (Lyons Press). Dusty does a fair amount of ghost hunting in her spare time and has seen some pretty odd stuff. So what does she think about ghosts and cats?

"Yes, I definitely think that cats can sense ghosts because they have more acute senses than people. They can see in the dark better and, because they can sense changes in magnetic fields and have more sensitive hearing, they're bound to notice ghosts," Dusty says. "In fact, I think cats are more sensitive to ghosts than dogs. I know of people whose cats follow something that's not there.

"It works on the same principle as animals that disappear before an earthquake. There were very few animals that died in the tsunami in 2005 because they sensed it and went to higher ground. It's the same principle. Animals have more awareness of things around them."

So, there you have it: If there are ghosts, you can bet your cat has met a couple.

Do cats have nine lives?

BOTH CAROLINE AND MAGGIE ARE convinced that cats have only one life on this planet, just like we do. And you probably would agree, unless you believe in reincarnation. So, where did this saying get started?

We don't really know, but the number 9 has held religious significance throughout the ages as being 3 times 3, by the Egyptians to the Celts to the Norse (and even the Christians, who worship the Trinity). Cat goddesses, Bastet and Sekhmet, were worshipped throughout Egypt, and the fact that cats were revered as having mystical powers may have something to do with those nine lives.

The nine lives thing may also be a consequence of the uncanny ability that cats possess to right themselves, even from great heights (but they don't always land on their feet, even if they try). This seemingly magical ability may have given cats the reputation of having more luck and possessing more magical qualities than they in fact do. But we think cats are pretty magical already, even without their nine lives. 🐾

Are black cats really unlucky?

YOU SEE A BLACK CAT DASH OUT ahead of you, and you hold your breath. What was that about black cats? Are they unlucky?

Stop holding your breath; you'll turn blue. You see, black cats aren't more unlucky than any other cat that might cross your path (unless you trip over it!), but history hasn't been kind to the cat whose color is black.

Black has been associated with evil, death, the devil, and witches (at least, wicked witches). Cats, especially black ones, were persecuted throughout the ages as being either demons or witches' familiars. Cats, being nocturnal, were also associated with other creatures of the night, like bats and wolves, both having their fright factors. And cats have those strangely shaped pupils that people associate with reptiles. So, black cats are doubly cursed and have been targeted for harm just because of their coat color.

Even nowadays, because of the black cats' bad press, life is hard on black cats. Black cats are usually overlooked when people adopt cats and kittens at shelters, even though they may have wonderful personalities. So, are black cats unlucky?

Yes, definitely. But only to themselves. 🐾

Why does clumping litter clump?

YOU REALLY HAVE TOO MUCH TIME on your hands if you've been wondering about this one. Basically, clumping litter is made from absorbent clay (sodium bentonite) that expands and globs together molecularly when you pour liquid into it. (Think, like dough.) When it dries out a bit, it will actually compact itself, forming a tight glob.

Staying up at night wondering about that, were you? 🐾

Why are there so many cats?

YOU SEE CATS EVERYWHERE. People are always giving away free kittens or cats to a good home. But why are there so many of them?

Much of it has to do with the cat's reproductive cycle. When a cat goes into estrus and mates, the act of mating stimulates ovulation, which almost always guarantees a pregnant cat. Combine that with about 70 million feral cats (according to the Humane Society of the United States) and the some 88.3 million pet cats (according to the American Pet Products Manufacturers Association) in the United States alone, and you can see how the number of cats can add up, especially if they're not spayed or neutered. 🐾

Can one cat and her offspring actually produce 420,000 cats in seven years?

CAN ONE CAT AND HER OFFSPRING produce 420,000 cats in a seven-year period? The number is truly staggering. You may have heard this statistic from various humane organizations. But how true is it?

Not likely, according to the *Feral Cat Times,* wherein a researcher and professor at North Carolina State reported that three-fourths of all feral kittens die before they reach reproductive age. Having some mathematicians at the University of Washington crunch the numbers, the results were surprising, to say the least. Assuming each female cat produces a litter of six kittens, of which three-fourths die, the number of cats produced over seven years would be ninety-nine cats, including the original cat.

If you really think about it, it makes a lot of sense. After all, with some 70 million feral cats, we'd not only be hip deep in cats here in the United States (figure that the population would have exploded to 14.7 trillion cats during a seven-year period, assuming half were female), but within less than a hundred years, we would have ended up creating such a kitty mass that not only would the mews be deafening, but the cats would have overrun everything, and probably the mass itself would have collapsed the earth into a very furry black hole. (Not likely, but fun to ponder.)

So, while cats are indeed busy procreating, they aren't *that* busy. Either that, or we have a lot more to worry about than a comet or asteroid hitting the earth or a super-volcano exploding.

Are cats psychic?

YOU'RE ABOUT TO LEAVE on a trip for a few days. Before you know it, your cat is moping around the house or acting anxious because she knows she's going to the boarding kennel. Is she psychic? Does she know when things are going to happen before they do?

Before you start calling your furry companion Karnack, you might consider a cat's amazing powers of observation that would put Sherlock Holmes to shame. Cats, being predators, are great observers and know the subtle signs that indicate when you're about to go on a trip, even before you pack your bags. Your cat notices the frequency of phone calls, your demeanor, your smell and mood, and other things that have cued her off in the past that you're leaving.

Your cat isn't psychic: She's just very good at recognizing the signs of things to come. 🐾

Is there a cat who is a furry Grim Reaper?

WE KNOW THAT ANIMALS ARE particularly sensitive to people. Dogs can actually sniff out cancer or tell people when they're going to have an epileptic seizure. But we were a bit surprised to find out that one cat may actually predict when people are going to die before they do.

The cat's name is Oscar, and as of this writing he has accurately predicted twenty-five deaths at a Providence, Rhode Island, nursing home and rehabilitation center. He checks out patients, and if any are going to pass away in the next few hours, he curls up beside them. He's often more accurate than the doctors. So, Oscar is watched very closely, and if any patients receive a tender visit from Oscar, the nursing home staff contacts the family so they may be with their loved one during the final hours.

Oscar's talent may or may not be unique, but he is the first of note. Some experts guess that he can smell a change in the patients that we humans can't. All we can say is that we really aren't too keen about Oscar showing up at our beds at odd hours of the night. 🐾

Do cats have souls and go to heaven?

THIS IS ARGUABLY ONE OF THE questions that will generate a fair amount of controversy for many years to come. In Christianity, especially Roman Catholicism, it was believed that animals—including cats—don't have souls and therefore don't go to heaven. This doctrine has pretty much been St. Thomas Aquinas' doing, although some versions of Christianity are coming around to accepting cats as having souls, thereby allowing them entry into heaven.

While the Catholic Church still wavers on its cat/soul/heaven questions, they do celebrate the feast day of St. Francis of Assisi with an annual blessing of the animals. Other religions, both past and present, do insist that animals (and therefore cats) have souls. Buddism, Hinduism, Shinto, Pagan (e.g., Wiccan), and many other non-Christian religions all treat animals as having souls.

But do they really have souls? For that matter, do you have a soul? Do I have a soul?

In truth, we may never know whether cats have souls; at least while we are still breathing.

What is cat scratch fever?

CAT SCRATCH FEVER OR, more correctly, cat scratch disease (CSD), is a bacterial disorder caused by *Bartonella henselae*. Most people who get it have been bitten or scratched by a cat. Children are often afflicted.

Symptoms of CSD include swollen lymph nodes, infection at the injury site, fever, headache, and lethargy. About 40 percent of all cats have this malady sometime in their life.

In most people, CSD is a minor ailment that goes away in time. However, people with more serious health problems or who are immune-compromised (due to HIV/AIDS, cancer, or organ transplants) can develop severe complications associated with infections.

Ways to prevent getting CSD are pretty straightforward: keep your cat's nails clipped, don't roughhouse with the cat, don't let your cat lick open sores, keep fleas to a minimum (fleas are shown to carry the bacteria), and wash any scratches or bites and apply antibiotic ointment on them. If you show symptoms, see your doctor. There are antibiotics to treat it.

Can a cat really cause problems
with a pregnancy (toxoplasmosis)?

IF YOU'RE A WOMAN WHO IS PREGNANT, you may have heard that you should get rid of your cat, for various reasons. One is that a cat can carry a disease called toxoplasmosis, which can cause retardation or blindness to the unborn infant when it is infected. So, if you own a cat, do you need to get rid of it when you become pregnant?

Absolutely not! While cats can carry toxoplasmosis, it's unlikely you will get infected by your cat. Here's why:

At least 30 percent of the human population has been infected with toxoplasmosis at one time, usually as a result of eating under-cooked meat, drinking contaminated water, or not practicing proper sanitation (e.g., eating after gardening or cleaning the litter box). If a woman has been infected once, before she became pregnant, her baby is not at risk should she come in contact with the organism again. In fact, most people are more likely to contract toxoplasmosis from eating uncooked meat than from their pets. Toxoplasmosis usually manifests itself in the form of flulike symptoms. You're likely to not even know you were infected with it. (It may be linked to schizophrenia, but there's no hard evidence there.)

In order for you to contract toxoplasmosis from your cat and harm your unborn baby, you would have to meet several requirements. You could never have been infected with toxoplasmosis before you became pregnant, plus your cat would have to contract toxoplasmosis while you were pregnant, and then you would have to eat some of the cat's fecal matter (eww!) while the cat was infected. Cats remain infected for no more than three weeks. Once the cat has been infected, he can't become infected again. So it's highly unlikely that you would contract toxoplasmosis from your cat—and just as unlikely that you would eat cat poop, unless you're really into that kind of thing. So, the chance of your getting toxoplasmosis from your kitty is pretty slim.

Even so, the U.S. Centers for Disease Control and Prevention (CDC) recommends that you keep your cat inside where she can't contract it. Have someone else scoop out and clean the litter box daily (or wear a mask and gloves if you have to do it yourself), but do it daily because it takes one to five days for the feces to become infected. Feeding your cat a diet of commercial cat food (no meat or scraps) is advisable. The CDC also recommends hand washing and proper sanitation, and cooking all your meat.

And don't lick the cat's litter box—that's clearly a no-no.

Did Edgar Allen Poe die from a rabid cat's bite?

A BITE FROM A RABID CAT? Could Edgar Allen Poe's death have been as creepy as his writings?

The famous poet and horror writer Edgar Allen Poe left this world by a death that has been a mystery even after 147 years. Poe died on October 7, 1849, at age thirty-nine. He was found unconscious in front of Ryan's Tavern in Baltimore, Maryland, on September 28 and brought to Washington College Hospital.

When Poe regained consciousness, he was delirious with tremors and hallucinations. Some sources state he could not drink water, although another says he could. When Poe died, the Baltimore Commissioner of Health, Dr. J. F. C. Handel, stated Poe's death as "congestion on the brain."

Poe was well known for having pets, especially cats, and one may have bitten him and transmitted rabies. An article in *Science* magazine of September 27, 1996, proposes this theory, and R. Michael Benitez, M.D. (a cardiologist at the University of Maryland Medical

Center) also believes that Poe died from rabies and published his ideas in the September 1996 issue of the *Maryland Medical Journal*.

This theory is one of many as to the cause of Poe's death. Other proposed causes of death include Poe's addiction to opiates and alcohol, epilepsy, diabetes, cholera, heart disease, tuberculosis, or possibly a group of ruffians beating up Poe and forcing him to vote for their candidate after plying him with alcohol (called "cooping"—a popular but illegal practice at that time).

We may never know the truth about Poe's death, mainly because experts are in disagreement here. If it were rabies, Poe's death would indeed have been as eerie as many of his writings.

Do cats really suck the life out of babies?

YOU'VE PROBABLY HEARD the story of how a cat can suck the breath from a baby and how you ought to get rid of your cat for that reason alone. To this, we say, nonsense—cats don't do that sort of thing.

The whole mess got started during the medieval era (although the earliest recorded written statements are dated to the early 1600s). This is one of those old wives' tales probably designed to explain the death of an infant (maybe from sudden infant death syndrome [SIDS]). It just so happens that the cat was there, and maybe sleeping with the baby (because cats like warm things), and the baby died. Cats made convenient scapegoats for all sorts of things, so why not the death of babies?

A number of corollary stories surround it, regarding how cats can actually smother people. And while we realize that having a cat lay on you can be pretty smothering, trust us: There is no malice aforethought or breath-sucking going on.

Are cats used in pagan sacrifices?

THIS QUESTION ODDLY enough caused much fervor in Maggie's LiveJournal when she asked Wiccan and Pagan friends about cat sacrifice. It appears that most Wiccans consider cats sacred, and that sacrificing a cat would violate their rede (guidelines): "An it harm none, do as thou wilt."

Most Wiccans believe that causing harm to others will cause harm to return to them threefold. Many Wiccans Maggie questioned say their cats often attend their ceremonies, and some actually join in. In most cases, stories of cruelty against animals are largely tales told by teenagers and wannabe Satanists. Wiccans, in fact, often encourage people to keep their cats safely indoors around Halloween to avoid cruel pranksters. 🐾

Do cats cause schizophrenia?

YOU MAY HAVE HEARD THERE is a possible link between cats and schizophrenia. (We're not talking about a cat acting schizo, we're talking about the actual disease in humans.) Several professors of psychology and several veterinarians have discerned a link between toxoplasmosis and schizophrenia in humans.

About 1 percent of the human population contracts schizophrenia. Dr. E. Fuller Torrey began to see parallels between cat ownership and schizophrenia and even discovered that there were no clear cases of the disease in a cat-free environment such as that of Papua, New Guinea. Torrey found that children raised with a cat had a 53 percent higher risk of schizophrenia (though breastfeeding conferred a 51 percent higher risk) than those who weren't. (A 200 percent higher risk is considered statistically significant.)

Dr. Milton H. McAllister, professor of pathobiology at the University of Illinois, College of Veterinary Medicine Urbana-Champaign, believes that there is a link between toxoplasmosis and schizophrenia.

So, what do you do? If you read our section on toxoplasmosis, you know already that you can get the disease from undercooked meat and poor hygiene (not to mention licking the cat's litter box). Keeping your cat or cats inside and feeding them a commercial diet reduces the chance of them contracting toxoplasmosis. Cleaning the litter box daily ensures that the cat's feces may not become infected.

So, while you may think that your cat is driving you crazy in many ways, a little care taken will make sure he won't drive you totally insane. 🐾

Is there really a cat called a twisty cat?

"TWISTY CATS" OR "TWISTY KATS" are names given a group of cats bred in Texas that have severe deformities of the wrist, known as radial hypoplasia, where the normally long bone between the elbow and wrist is drastically shortened, or even missing, and the paws are deformed and pointing to the sides.

Only a few people are responsible for twisty cats, claiming that they are the so-called perfect cat because they can't climb, run, or claw things. These cats are quite controversial because the original breeder deliberately bred in a severe deformity. Because twisty cats can't use their forearms, they must hop on their hind legs kangaroo-style, or crawl using their wrists instead of 2 front paws. Twisty cats would not be able to survive or breed without human intervention, having this severe deformity.

While twisty cats exist, there is no viable breed associated with them. Most cat owners and breeders consider breeding these cats to be cruel. The Cat Fanciers' Association (CFA) does not regard these cats as a breed, and twisty cats would fail to meet their guidelines regarding a healthy breed. 🐾

Can cats get the plague?

WE'VE ALL HEARD ABOUT bubonic plague (the Black Death) from history books, but you might not know whether cats are resistant to plague or not. Plague is caused by the bacteria *Yersinia pestis* and is carried by fleas on rodents. Animals, such as cats, can become infected by eating infected rodents. So yes, they can. And they can become carriers of the plague themselves. 🐾

Did a cat really climb the Matterhorn?

MOUNTAIN CLIMBING ISN'T for the faint of heart, which brings us to the daring deeds of a kitten owned by Josephine Aufdenblatten of Geneva. On September 6, 1950, this four-month-old kitty had the heart and expertise of a mountain climber and followed an expedition led by Edmund Biner to the top of the Matterhorn, a peak in Switzerland that rises 14,691 feet high.

No doubt, the climbers took pity on this little guy because they scooped him up and gave him a ride back down in their backpacks. 🐾

Did a cat really rescue her kittens from a fire?

IN MARCH 1996, firefighters were called to a garage fire in Brooklyn, New York. As they finished putting out the fire, one of the firefighters noticed a mother calico cat carrying her kittens to safety. She was badly scorched, and the firefighter rescued her and her six kittens and brought them to North Shore Animal League in Port Washington, New York. The cat was named Scarlett because she was severely burned.

Sadly, one kitten didn't make it, but the other kittens and Scarlett all survived. They were adopted out to loving homes where they lived on in comfort. 🐾

Are there really cats with two faces?

YOU MAY HAVE HEARD SOMETHING on the news about kittens being born with two faces. Is this really a condition?

Actually, it is. In fact, conjoined animals (often called Siamese twins) are nothing new in the animal world, and certainly aren't new with cats. Some cats with two faces are actually conjoined twins, but many cats are two-faced due to viruses or even a protein that disrupts the embryo's growth.

Two-faced cats are uncommon, and most don't live very long after birth, usually only three or four days at most. 🐾

Are cats eaten as food anywhere?

YOU MAY HAVE HEARD HORROR stories about cats being eaten as food in places such as China, Korea, and Vietnam. Is this true?

Sad to say, yes it is. In some parts of China, Korea, and Vietnam, cats are looked on as food, especially in southern China, where cat thighs are made into meatballs. These animals are often killed inhumanely and in view of others awaiting their fate.

But there is a growing humane movement even within these countries to stop this ritual. Not all people consider cats food items and are as repulsed as we are by this practice. 🐾

Will plastic jugs filled with water keep cats from pooping on your lawn?

IN A WORD, NO. Not unless you plan on covering your entire lawn with them. 🐾

Is cat litter radioactive?

DOES YOUR KITTY GLOW IN THE DARK? Well, if she does, you may be thinking about that story you heard that cat litter is radioactive.

Rest assured, unless someone starts dumping uranium in cat litter, cat litter isn't radioactive. The story got started as a sarcastic joke from a quip on *NBC Nightly News* in 1997 that backfired and caused consternation among pet owners.

Unless your cat is ingesting radioactive isotopes (like those found in a lab test), there's no reason to suspect radioactive litter.

Unless your kitty really does glow in the dark.

Is cocoa mulch harmful to pets?

A NEW PRODUCT IN LAWN and garden shops is cocoa bean shell mulch. It's biodegradable and uses products that would normally be thrown away. But is it safe for pets?

The answer is, no. Cocoa mulch is highly toxic to pets because it contains high amounts of theobromine, the same toxin found in chocolate.

So, skip the cocoa mulch and use bark if you must mulch.

When was cat litter invented?

CAT LITTER WAS INVENTED by Edward Lowe in 1947. His neighbor, Kay Draper, was trying to use ash as kitty litter, and he suggested Fuller's Earth, an absorbent clay used at his father's company. Lowe tried to have the local pet store sell five-pound bags of kitty litter, but since sand for cat boxes was so cheap, Lowe suggested to the pet store owner to give the product away. People were hooked and soon began purchasing kitty litter.

In 1964, Edward Lowe's brand of Tidy Cat appeared on grocery store shelves. And as they say, the rest is history.

What was the oldest cat?

THE OLDEST CAT WAS A ginger-and-white tomcat named Spike, who was born in 1970 when his owner, David Elkington (age seven at the time) bought Spike from a market for two shillings. Spike lived two months past his thirty-first birthday in Bridport, Dorset, England, making him the world's oldest cat on record. 🐾

11

CAT
DOMESTICATION

When did the cat get domesticated?

CATS HAVE BEEN HANGING OUT with humans for quite some time. Maybe not as long as dogs, but archeological evidence shows that cats were buried with people at least 9,500 years ago. A grave site in the Neolithic village of Shillourokambos (say that one three times fast) on Cyprus has a human buried presumably with a pet cat along with polished stones, seashells, and other artifacts. This demonstrates the close relationship that apparently existed between humans and cats 4,000 years before the Egyptians painted their image on walls.

There are suggestions of cats being domesticated much earlier. Some Stone Age pottery from 10,000 years ago depicts cats. If that weren't enough, new DNA evidence suggests that the link between cats and humans may extend back as far as 130,000 years.

How cool is that? 🐾

How did the cat get domesticated?

THIS BRINGS US TO THE big question of how cats got domesticated in the first place. Most experts believe that cats were pretty much self-domesticating, that is, they knew a good thing when they saw it and decided to hang around us humans for easy meals. But that didn't happen overnight. Cats are pretty territorial and move only when they have to (through pressure or because humans bring them along).

You see, humans had to make the transition from a hunter-gatherer society to an agrarian society for the cat to become truly domesticated. The moment we started growing grains (which brought in the vermin, such as mice and rats), the cat's domestication was assured. Cats, in their never-ending quest for fast food, found that humans were pretty useful for attracting their prey species. So cats that could tolerate humans stuck around, hunted mice and rats, and made little cats that could tolerate humans. Because of the ample prey supply, tame cats did better than their wild counterparts, thus paving the way for domestication.

At some point, humans took notice of these helpful critters and brought them into their homes as pets and guardians. 🐾

What is the ancestor to the cat, and where do cats come from?

DNA EVIDENCES SUGGESTS that the cat's ancestor was the North African wildcat or *Felis silvestris lybica*. No other wildcats, with the exception of an occasional cross with the European wildcat, are evident in the domestic cat.

Genetic data suggest that cats domesticated themselves in the area known as the Fertile Crescent, that is, where Iraq, Syria, Lebanon, and Israel sit. Egyptians seem to have raised domestication of cats to an art form, if not to a science. 🐾

INDEX

and cats. Her writing awards have included the Dog Writers' Association of America's Maxwell Award (three times), the Pet Sitters' International First Canine Award, and second place in the 2005 Preditors and Editors People's Choice Awards. She is the author of many pet books including *Introduction to Dog Agility* (Barron''s Educational Series), *A Dog's Wisdom* and *The Complete Guide to Mutts* (Howell Book House), and *The Pocket Idiot's Guide to Homemade Dog Food* (Alpha Books).

Maggie is a member of the Dog Writers' Association of America and the Cat Writers' Association. She is a pet behaviorist and has trained over 50 dogs in obedience, agility, backpacking, and sledding sports. She has appeared on dozens of radio programs and in hundreds of magazines and newspapers as a pet expert. Her writing has appeared in *Prevention Magazine, Dog Fancy, Dog World, Mushing Magazine* and has been syndicated across the Internet through various newspapers.

When she's not working with dogs or cats, she writes science fiction and fantasy including *Prophecy of Swords, Runestone of Teiwas, Lachlei, The King's Champion*, and the upcoming werewolf thriller *Howling Dead.*

Encyclopedia of Dog Breeds (Barrons Educational) *Is Your Dog?* and *Silly Dog Tricks* (Sterling Publishing). Her work has won many awards, including several awards for their scientific and health content.

Caroline's research and teaching interests revolve around canine behavior, senses, and genetics. She has served as a canine consultant to the FAA and is on the AKC Canine Health Foundation President's Council.

Caroline has lived with dogs and cats (Siamese, Domestic Shorthairs, and Oriental Shorthairs) almost all of her life. She attended her first cat show when she was nine years old and it was her fascination with them that led her to ask questions about their behavior and, especially, senses. Those questions eventually led to her PhD, with subsequent research and teaching interests revolving around domestic animal behavior, senses, and genetics. Of course, cats always want to show just how foolish such attempts to understand them are, so she is regularly put in her place by them!